FlexScore

Financial Advice for the Rest of Us

Jeff Burrow, CFP® & Jason Gordo, AIF®

Fat Donkey Publishing

© 2013 by Jason M. Gordo and Jeffrey S. Burrow

Published by Fat Donkey Publishing

156 2nd Street, San Francisco, Ca. 94105

First Printing March 2013

ISBN# 987-0-9890558-0-2

Printed in the United States of America

10 9 8 7 6 5 4 3 2 1

Library of Congress Control Number: 2013933700

Information and examples presented in this book are for educational purposes only and should not be construed as specific financial or investment advice.

Cover Design: Marcia Herrmann Design

Authors' Back Cover Photo: Melissa Cohoon-Neece, Logo M Photography

FlexScore

Financial Advice for the Rest of Us

Page 101 ~ Chapter Six

Why Your Current 'Advisor' Has Never Done This For You

Page 113 ~ Chapter Seven

What's Your Direction: What Matters and What Doesn't?

Page 145 ~ Chapter Eight

What Does It Mean If Your Score Sucks?

Page 171 ~ Chapter Nine

Can I Retire Before Hitting 1,000?

Page 185 ~ Chapter Ten

How FlexScore Helps You Avoid Common Financial Failures

Page 211 ~ Chapter Eleven

Success Stories of FlexScore in Action

Page 241 ~ About the Authors

TABLE OF CONTENTS

ACKNOWLEDGEMENTS

PAGE 1 ~ INTRODUCTION
'Your Financial Life as You Understand it and Want it to be'

PAGE 9 ~ CHAPTER ONE
Money Can Make You Happy

PAGE 27 ~ CHAPTER TWO
You're Wealthier Than You Think (Maybe)

PAGE 49 ~ CHAPTER THREE
What is FlexScore, How Does It Work & How Do You Know Your Score?

PAGE 69 ~ CHAPTER FOUR
Everyone's FlexScore is Different

PAGE 79 ~ CHAPTER FIVE
Financial Independence is For Everyone

We can't thank Michael Zagaris enough. Without his mentorship, friendship and occasional "kick in the butt," FlexScore would continue residing among our "big book of business ideas." His gentle nudges challenged us to go do it. Mike told us to take the road less traveled, and we have.

We are grateful to Dan Costa and his mentorship. His openness to being a "sounding board" for our business ideas allowed us to be confident and sure in our decision to launch FlexScore. Dan challenged us to "find a hole and fill it." FlexScore does just that.

There have been countless others who have helped us along the way and to them we say, thank you.

Now here are some personal acknowledgements.

From Jason: To my high school sweetheart, best friend and wife Tracy, I love you. Each and every day you are an amazing mother to our beautiful daughters, Emily, Lily and Grace, a wonderful wife to me and a great friend to so many. Thank you for allowing me to chase my dreams.

To the Gordo Girls, you are the greatest gift I have ever received. You are all special to me and I am proud to be your dad. I love you.

To my business partner, Jeff Burrow, without whom all I'd have are big dreams, thank you for asking all of the "have you thought about this" questions. You make me better all the time. I appreciate your partnership and thank you for making things happen.

From Jeff: To my dedicated and inspiring wife who has been by my side through thick and thin, I love and appreciate you. To my kids, Bronson, Makayla and Kendall, this book is that "work thing" I've had going on for so long. You are the reason I want to financially change this country, one person at a time. When you grow up, my hope is that you won't ever have to struggle financially because of poor decisions made by the people who came before you.

ACKNOWLEDGEMENTS

This book was written for the average American as well as the financial advisor community. It is full of lessons and stories of real client situations, both successes and failures. We think it is time for real industry change and believe FlexScore* brings it. Our hope is that readers will use this book, and FlexScore, to become financially secure, gain insight into our industry and find out ways to improve *their* FlexScores. At the end of the day, this is just a book. It's up to you to take action towards your own financial progress.

Without the trust and confidence of our clients, our business would not exist today. Our focus will continue to be client driven and aimed at better helping people accomplish their financial goals. Our clients helped create the idea of FlexScore. FlexScore was born out of the thousands of client conversations we've had over the years. We appreciate them and their commitment to our company.

We are grateful to Adam Zagaris and Melroy Saldanha, our co-founders. Their individual strengths have improved our concept and we are honored to call each of them our friend. Together we will do great things.

We get to work with an amazing group of people every day at Valley Wealth Inc., our financial planning and investment management firm in Modesto, California. It's often said that people make the difference, and ours actually do. We are impressed with the dedication and loyalty they show our clients. Thank you Dezaree, Allen, Mark R., Linda, Karen, Mark S., Joel and Audrey for your significant contributions to our company.

*FlexScore is a Registered Trademark of Fat Donkey, Inc., founded by Jason Gordo and Jeff Burrow.

To my business partner, Jason Gordo, we've continually heard that partnerships don't always work out. Egos can get in the way. Greed can become divisive. Despite those warnings, we've got a good thing going. Thank you. Let's keep it up.

Finally, we would both like to thank our friend Marc Grossman, a Sacramento writer, who kept us on track and turned our idea of a book into a reality.

FlexScore: *Financial Advice for the Rest of Us*

'Your Financial Life as You Understand it and Want it to be'

Until now a person only had three options when attempting to figure out the state of her financial life: Go it alone, hire a financial advisor or simply bury her head in the sand. Unfortunately, most people select the latter option and find themselves lost in the financial wilderness. Enter FlexScore.

FlexScore is a revolutionary tool that gives every person financial clarity. FlexScore is an entirely new service empowering people to take more control over their financial lives.

FlexScore is not your daddy's financial advisor. It doesn't wear a suit. It's never played the back nine or collected nice Scotch. It doesn't drive a BMW, smoke cigars or drink martinis over lunch.

Your FlexScore is a number that encompasses everything you own, everything you owe and everything you're doing with your money—all based on the goals you set for yourself.

FlexScore "gameifies" financial planning; it turns financial planning into a game. FlexScore consists of a point system, with 1,000 being the maximum number of points you can earn. It awards points that reward you for doing the right thing with your money based on the goals you yourself set. It takes away points for practices that detract from meeting your goals. By doing so it also makes the process fun, which is part of the genius of FlexScore.

Your FlexScore number is the summation of the past financial decisions that got you where you are today. Your financial situation is dynamic and ever changing, and you should be the person controlling its movements. If you're not, then who is?

FlexScore provides an easy-to-understand way for you to visualize and gauge your overall financial health. A person's finances can be complicated. There are mortgages, 401(k) retirement plans, stock portfolios, life insurance...and much more. It is difficult for the majority of people to properly assess how all of these things come together and fit into the "big picture" of their lives.

But FlexScore goes beyond just showing you how you're doing. It also tells you specifically how to improve. It gives you the practical and easy to follow steps you should take to achieve your goals.

FlexScore is becoming the language of the neighborhood because of its simplicity, transparency and flexibility.

Everyone has unique goals, and your FlexScore reflects the uniqueness that is you. It will help you manage both your short- and long-term financial goals without neglecting either one. Whether you want to buy a home, save for retirement, pay down student loans or get out of debt, FlexScore helps you make it happen.

What are those things you really want to do with your money—or think maybe you should be doing—but you really don't know how? FlexScore gets that monkey off your back by telling you what to do and how to get it done.

FlexScore is a tool on the Web that you can visit at home or from a mobile device. You can look at it while you work, while you shop, while you eat or while you talk on the phone. The more you use FlexScore, the clearer your financial picture becomes.

Your FlexScore number will generate your own set of customized action steps. Acting on those steps will move you forward—and improve your FlexScore. That number will keep you continually engaged in your own financial life. As your number goes up, your financial life will get better.

You can check how well you're doing anytime, anywhere. Keep up to date with monthly emails from FlexScore that track your progress. Learn how to reach your goals more quickly with free advice and tailored action steps. Improve your situation by improving your financial literacy by utilizing FlexScore's Learning Center.

Want to have a little money available each month to further your financial goals? FlexScore shows you how. Then, when you have that extra money available monthly, FlexScore shows you whether it's better to use it to pay off debt or to sock it away for the future. Because FlexScore is a holistic view of your finances, it shows you which choices do more for you at any given time.

FlexScore is the financial equivalent of an MRI (magnetic resonance imaging) machine that gives doctors a 360-degree view of your body. MRIs are an invaluable aid in medical diagnoses and in saving lives. FlexScore accomplishes the same thing for your financial life, offering a 360-degree examination of everything having to do with your finances. It singles out problems, suggests meaningful actions to take and continuously monitors progress, thus helping you better achieve your goals.

FlexScore keeps your focus on those aspects of your financial life you can control: How much money you can put away. How much debt you should pay down. How to invest your money. And how to adequately protect your loved ones.

Here is what FlexScore is not.

It is not vague analysis.

It is not an insurance agent overselling you insurance products for his benefit and not yours.

It is not a stockbroker making big commissions each time your money moves around.

It is not a confusing, overpriced financial advisor who repeats the mantra, "Just stay the course and everything will be fine… in the long run." What if you aren't even on the right course to begin with? Wouldn't that be good to know now?

It is not a static picture of your net worth without any accompanying understandable advice on how to do better.

FlexScore is not some phony 10-step program concocted by a self-proclaimed financial guru.

We're just two guys who began our careers working for a large Wall Street brokerage firm. Over time we came to realize that Wall Street, as an industry, is focused on salesmanship. We founded our own independent financial services firm because we wanted a practice focused on stewardship, and on placing our clients' needs ahead of our own.

We created FlexScore based on our experience that when people undertake the long form method of traditional financial planning, adhering to six steps based on sound industry standards, they achieve their financial goals more often, more effectively and in a manner that pleasantly surprises them. Most people are afraid of this process until we sit down and take them through it. No wonder: It's a process they don't understand and that has always been foreign to them. In our one-on-one sessions with clients we remove the mystery and intimidation involving financial planning while respecting the basic integrity of the method. FlexScore can accomplish the same thing for the masses of people in America who don't sit down regularly or at all with personal financial advisors. That's why we call it "financial advice for the rest of us."

FlexScore is straight-talking, Wall Street lingo-free financial advice. It's your friend and trusted companion. We've deconstructed the old-fashioned financial advice model and reconstructed it with you in mind. Comprehensive. Simple. Understandable. Accessible. Fun.

Here is a sampling of just some of the ground this book covers that will make FlexScore all the more relevant and important in your daily life.

- Remember the metaphor about the race between the

tortoise and the hare? Much of our grandparents' generation selected the tortoise. Many from our generation chose the hare. We often expect to get money quickly and believe the avenue to wealth is taking big risks. But making long-term financial progress means taking a middle ground: A good measure of disciplined savings plus taking some appropriate risk. Mostly, it demands a degree of steadiness or staying the course.

- By focusing too much on what other people have, too many of us try to achieve things we don't need. You know, keeping up with the Joneses. Instead, we need to focus on our own perspective by deciding where we want to go financially and then how to survive from the 1st to the 30th of each month so there will be some money left over to further the goals we set. Financial life then becomes a lot less burdensome since we're concentrating on what we really need (as opposed to what we think we should want) and on those things that are within our control to achieve. FlexScore is the key to helping us come to these realizations for ourselves.

- A key feature of FlexScore is peer ranking. Would you like to know where you stand in relation to people your age, with your income, and living in your area? This is much better than keeping up with the Joneses. It will motivate you to do the right things for yourself and your family.

- It is easy, and all too common, for people to put off saving or investing towards retirement. They forget the biggest single risk for people once they stop working: Running out of money before they run out of life.

- Your financial path is determined by the choices you make. If you choose based on what makes you feel good now instead of what you need to do for your future, you can end up wanting (or craving) retirement some day but lacking the ability to do so. Determining your FlexScore and regularly keeping it in sight, having it stare you in the face, will supply you with the top-of-mind awareness required to achieve your goals by constantly making informed, objective decisions. Hopefully, you will then be able to decide when, and under what circumstances, you will stop working.

• Becoming financially independent is a common goal for nearly everyone. You may not be able to achieve it now, but you can work to do so at some point in your life. FlexScore will help you get there.

• Time is just as potent a resource as money. It is the greatest asset anyone can possess.

• Ignorance is not bliss, in life as well as in finances. Being financially ignorant is the surest way to ensure you will never be financially stress free.

• One reason FlexScore is so valuable is that it refocuses attention away from the investment markets you can't control and properly directs it to those items of financial necessity in your life that you *can* control.

• People harbor many common fallacies about investment, risk and debt that frequently foster very bad financial decisions and behaviors. Consistency is the key to success in investing; it's important to earn a consistent rate of return on your investments. It's also important to consistently save so you have the wherewithal to invest. For you to be able to save and grow your money, it's important to consistently work towards digging yourself out of debt and stay there so you aren't constantly wasting your money by paying back other people for using *their* money.

• Plenty of people who first begin using FlexScore earn a relatively low score. So the sinking feeling in your gut that you haven't been doing the right things financially all these years is probably justified. How can you improve your FlexScore? Is it ever too early or too late to start? What if there isn't enough time? Can you restart your financial life? Can you go back and redo what you've done or haven't done over many years or even decades? These are just some of the questions we address.

There are numerous examples throughout this book taken

from experiences we've had working with our clients. In these cases, we have changed the names and altered some of the circumstances to protect their privacy. We describe both smart and dumb decisions people have made with their money. In addition, we end the book with two chapters offering case studies of both types of people from different ages and walks of life. Readers will be able to identify in these examples commonplace financial mistakes they have made, as well as successes that can be theirs by using FlexScore.

www.FlexScore.com

CHAPTER ONE

Money *Can* Make You Happy

*"Money only buys a small measure of happiness and then
only for those who have the wisdom to use it properly."*

—Steven Scott, author and entrepreneur

Can money buy you happiness? It depends. In our combined experience of spending 27 years advising clients about their financial affairs, we have found that many of them, in our opinion, have enough money to make them happy. But the feeling of having enough money is a matter of personal perspective. It seems for a lot of people, the more money they have the higher they raise the hurdle on what they need. Even when people reach their financial goals and become satisfied having a certain amount of money, they begin comparing themselves to others and soon lose sight of their original mindset.

A neurosurgeon client of ours makes $600,000 a year; but he constantly complains about not having enough money in his retirement account. The reason is simple: This doctor spends more money than he takes in every year. This illustrates a basic fundamental of financial planning. If you make $50,000 a year, you're better served by spending less than that. If you earn $600,000 a year, you're better served spending less than that. If you spend as much or more than you make, you will never achieve financial security or increase your net worth. That is a key lesson from *The Millionaire Next Door: The Surprising Secrets of America's Wealthy,* a 1996 book by Thomas J. Stanley and William D. Danko examining a compilation of research on millionaires in America, those with $1 million or more in net assets, excluding the value of any home equity.

A similar point was made in the October 8, 2012 edition of the New Yorker magazine. Leon Cooperman, billionaire founder of the Omega Advisors hedge fund, related a visit from a world-respected 72-year old cardiologist and his wife, also a successful physician, who turned to Cooperman for personal financial advice. The couple's combined net worth was $10 million. Yet, "it was shocking how tight he was going to be in retirement," said Cooperman, who despite his vast wealth lives very modestly. "He needed $400,000 a year to live on. He had a home in Florida, a home in New Jersey. He had certain habits he wanted to continue to pursue." Ten million dollars was "not an impressive amount of capital for two people [who] were leading physicians for their entire work life." (Obviously, a large chunk of this physician's net worth was not producing income for him since a $10 million nest egg would typically be more than enough to produce an income higher than $400,000. He should've used FlexScore.)

Too many people compare their financial situation and their lifestyle to that of their friends or neighbors. For them it's all about keeping up with the Joneses. So they're always looking to trade up to a better house. Or they buy a newer and more expensive car every few years. They do it because it makes them *feel* better.

This physician client of ours was getting a decent enough return on his investments in the stock market. But he was getting increasingly frustrated with what he saw as the slow rate of return. He thought the answer to his financial problems was taking more risk. He has a relatively small amount of money in his retirement plan for someone who pulls down as much income as he does. Retirement accounts don't inherently come with much risk or illiquidity; if needed you can be as aggressive as you'd like. However, instead of investing his money in a field such as medicine that he knows something about, the surgeon put his funds into highly speculative, illiquid investments involving subjects about which he knew little or nothing.

So far as we know, his money is completely tied up. He can't access it and he isn't getting a much better rate of return than if he had the money in a traditional retirement plan. We can't say this is necessarily a bad deal, although we've seen many stories like this that don't end very well. If you put $100,000 of your money into speculative mining rights in Nevada, you could turn it into $300,000 (or something much less than you put in) over a period of time. In the meantime, your money is illiquid; if you change your mind or your financial circumstances suddenly change, you're stuck.

The fact remains that this physician has consistently earned a very high income for more than 15 years. Unfortunately, it has produced very little for him because of his spending habits and, more importantly, his financial perspective. He views himself as a medical professional. That requires him to maintain a certain sort of lifestyle: a doctor's lifestyle.

We've run across numerous people from an array of professions who receive high incomes, greater than $250,000 a year, and don't have much to show for them. They sport big home mortgages and fancy cars (with fancy car payments), take luxurious annual vacations and regularly go on expensive shopping sprees. They journey to San Francisco for $200 haircuts that can be had just as well where we live in Modesto, California for much less. Yet they've achieved little when it comes to putting their income into what we call "money-for-the-future" accounts.

Contrast the story of this doctor with another one of our clients who hails from the opposite end of the economic spectrum. She is not much younger than our physician, an immigrant from Mexico and a single mother raising three children by herself. She works at a local tomato processing facility where she has been steadily employed for more than 25 years. All that time she has consistently lived below her means on modest blue-collar wages. She has also consistently taken seriously the most basic financial responsibility: Contributing on a consistent and systematic basis a certain percentage of her pre-tax income into her company's 401(k) retirement plan. Today she has a little more than $400,000 in her retirement account, far outpacing what the doctor has built up.

The physician thinks of himself as financially sophisticated. The reality is quite different. In practice, the surgeon isn't as financially savvy as the immigrant worker. All the working woman did was trust the advice of the people around her at the plant who have done well by continually putting their money away into safe investments for their retirement.

We have served as financial advisors to this company and its employees for several years. When we first met with this lady, she voiced several concerns. The first was, "I don't know at this point in my life whether I will ever have enough money to retire some day and live a decent life."

The doctor assumed that because he enjoys such a high income he will have plenty of resources upon his retirement. The immigrant woman had been contributing into the 401(k) plan at her plant for some time before we arrived on the scene, but wasn't sure she was doing the right thing. She was just following the lead of her co-workers and those she viewed as successful, especially the facility's owners. She was grateful to have the job. Her thinking was that, if the people who own the processing plant think it's a good idea to put money away, then she should follow their example, since they're clearly doing well enough to own the place.

The doctor had the ability to put far more money away than the blue-collar worker, but choose not to do so in order to maintain his affluent lifestyle. "I'll always have a lot of money," is the surgeon's expectation. "I'm afraid I'm not saving enough," is the worker's worry. It turns out the immigrant was way ahead of the doctor. It had everything to do with the difference in their financial perspectives.

The other questions the woman at the tomato plant asked us were, "Am I saving enough money and putting it in the right place?" "Yes, absolutely," we answered.

The physician never asked these questions even though he earned so much more than the worker, and will never be able to retire at his present lifestyle unless his financial views and practices change. At the end of the day, the doctor will be forced to work longer than he had hoped or planned. The worker will be able to retire much sooner, and to a better lifestyle than she currently has.

Money does make you happy once you have enough of it to fulfill your basic needs and then some–so you can also have some fun.

The national household median income is just under $50,000 a year, according to a 2010 comprehensive study on income and poverty by the U.S. Census Bureau. A family can live comfortably on that income in many communities, much less so in others. It all depends on where people live and the lifestyle to which they are accustomed. Our doctor client would not be able to survive, given his present circumstances, on an annual income of $50,000. Our worker client would probably be delighted if she could spend that much in retirement and no longer have to work. A survey in 2012 by the Marist Institute for Public Opinion argued that making $50,000, the median annual income reported by the Census Bureau, could make most people genuinely happy.

Too many men and women can't even identify the amount of money they need to get from the 1st of the month to the 30th of the month. While there is no real word to describe this critical figure, we call it the "magical amount." It comprises the amount of money that would need to be magically deposited into your checking account on the first of the month to satisfy all your needs through the end of the month.

Let's say you need $4,000 a month on which to live. Here's how you know if that amount of money will make you happy: If you work your entire life and need $4,000 a month to live but all you can muster is $3,000 a month when you retire, you will not be happy. You will be forced to accept a lower quality lifestyle.

So, can money make you happy? Having enough to meet your needs will make you happy. But interestingly enough, having more than you need won't necessarily make you happier. The imperative here is being able to articulate–along with your spouse or loved ones--the amount you need. It shouldn't just cover the bare necessities; you want to have a little left over to be able to enjoy life too.

This will never be more important than when you retire and have the rest of your life ahead of you, which today is growing longer thanks to the miracles of modern medical science and healthier living habits. But enjoying your retirement requires that you save for it.

The Federal Reserve releases a study each year on how much the typical American saves. Average household savings crested at roughly 11 percent of income each year during the early 1980s. Today, it's at about three percent. Keep in mind that 2008 was the first year since the Great Depression or ever that average American households actually saved less than zero; they spent more than they took in. After the deep recession hit in 2008, Americans began saving more, but that trend appears to have peaked and seems to have trailed downward again. In any event, our saving as a nation is still a long way from where it once was or needs to be.

Sheldon Garon is a professor of history and East Asian studies at Princeton University and the author of a recent book, *Beyond Our Means: Why America Spends While the World Saves.* He said Americans became active savers mainly during World War II, when buying U.S. Savings Bonds in support of the war effort was seen as patriotic. The trend continued in the decades following the war. What happened to change that? Garon cited such causes as the mushrooming availability of mortgage and home equity loans, and consumer credit. Deregulation of the credit card industry followed a 1978 U.S. Supreme Court ruling eliminating interest rate caps on unpaid balances. That prompted credit card firms to intensively market their products, often to unsuspecting (or deliberately oblivious) consumers eager to assume more debt in the pursuit of "easy money."

The generational change in people's financial perceptions is palpable. Our grandparents who survived the Depression scrimped, saved and sacrificed, often just to survive. They got up early every morning and worked hard all day—when they could find work. Perhaps they started a small business and built it up. They made a better life for their children, who didn't have to endure the same hardships and were able to pursue an education. The second generation, our parents, benefited from the good fortune that came out of their grandparents' hard work. Perhaps our parents took over and became good stewards of the family business and did well.

Then the third generation came along. We didn't have to endure the struggles our grandparents experienced or the forbearance displayed by our parents. Too many members of the third generation have abandoned the values that encouraged their ancestors to save and build wealth from the ground up. Jason's grandfather grew up in a tent in the Yosemite Valley during the Depression. He knew what it meant to put food on the table, shelter over his head and clothes on his back. The trials and tribulations it took to possess those most basic essentials were not lost on him. As a young man, he experienced success in business. When he began having children, they didn't need to bear the same hardships; they benefited from the fruits of their father's labor. They were able to sleep in a bed with a roof over their heads, have decent clothes and food in the refrigerator, and pursue their educations. Their basic needs were met, and then some, with little effort on their part. Gen3 began life in an even better place. Each generation enjoyed more affluence than its parents knew, and each generation became more and more removed from the hardships of the 1930s and '40s.

The way Gen3, and now Gen4 (our children), earns and spends money is very different from Gen1. What was true of many individual families became increasingly true of the nation. We just expected to continue to prosper financially as a country--until recently.

All of a sudden we're not doing so well, as individuals and as a country, since the Great Recession hit. It's perplexing and deeply troubling for many. The 20- and 30-something-year-olds of today don't realize the discipline and hard work involved in creating and preserving the financial security and stability many families came to take for granted. What has been called the "Greatest Generation" knew it all too well. Those legacies have not been very effectively passed down to the next generation.

Still, not all financial beliefs from the Depression era are relevant now. There has to be a happy medium between how the Greatest Generation behaved towards money and how we behave towards it today. Talking with people from our grandparents' generation, you quickly understand that most of them were extremely risk averse. They only deposited their money in banks after New Deal reforms regulated practices and insured deposits. They bought savings bonds and later CDs while placing their money in savings and retirement accounts. They viewed saving as a means to an end.

Today there is the expectation that money will come to us quickly, that we can get wealthy overnight and that the way to get there--the means to the end--is to take big risks.

Applying the metaphor of the race between the tortoise and the hare, our grandparents' generation chose the tortoise; our generation favors the hare.

However, building long-term financial success requires the

right mix of disciplined savings, appropriate risk and also some steadiness in staying the course.

People often don't save enough because they don't believe saving money will make them happy. They worry saving will actually be harmful, depriving them of money they need in their everyday lives to do the things they want to do now.

Particularly in today's economy, when many people have had to make do with less, those who know what it feels like to lack money should get over the fear that saving will negatively alter their lifestyle. They must understand that this fear of not having enough money will be fully realized if they don't start saving. It's a trade off: A little bit of short-term pain to avoid a lot of long-term pain, which will happen if they stop working and haven't provided for enough income to sustain the lifestyle they knew when they were working. Any straight-thinking person will accept that trade off if he or she really "gets" what's involved.

We hear people tell us all the time that they can't afford to save. We tell them they can't afford not to.

We took on a couple as clients about a decade ago. The husband is a sales representative. The wife is an elementary school teacher. They are typical Middle Americans. They were in their late 20s at the time and hadn't yet started having kids. The wife has a public pension, none of which she can tap until retirement. The husband has a 401(k) plan through his employer into which both he and the employer contribute.

They already had the right desire and mindset to provide for the future, but they turned to us because they didn't know how to get started.

They had just paid off their college loans. They always had some kind of savings for the future. In addition, they had their "slush fund," a small pot of money into which they could dip if the refrigerator broke down or to pay for a better vacation. If they bought a new car, they'd keep it for 10 years instead of getting a new model every few years. They were models of financial common sense.

We set up accounts for the couple so they could put more into Roth IRAs. Once the children came, we established accounts for their kids' college educations. The goal was not for the parents to cover 100 percent of college costs, but to be able to substantially subsidize them. It's commendable, we pointed out, for mothers and fathers to help their children, but not to the extent that college savings accounts undermine the capacity to contribute into retirement accounts.

This couple jokes to themselves about how they're always pinching pennies. They may think they do, but they really have a very nice life now. They can go out to eat and take a couple of vacations each year. They do many family activities together. What they don't do is anything extravagant or pursue things that are not well planned or thought out. They also don't buy anything on credit. That's a big deal.

The burden of debt saddles families with demands that they allocate more of their income to pay off that debt, which they must do if they ever hope to achieve financial freedom. If you retire your debt or never take it on, as this couple has done, you free up hundreds of dollars a month to use for today–and tomorrow.

This couple also does something else that is smart: They never let friends or neighbors guide how they spend their money or live their lives. They're definitely not trying to keep up with the Joneses. They know exactly what they want in their lives. That's the frame of reference through which they always make financial decisions. Consequently, they've done very well for themselves, boasting two wonderful kids and no debt on the salaries of a salesman and a teacher.

Not only will they be able to retire at age 60, but they will also have more than enough money to live their current lifestyle–and even be able to spoil their grandchildren, donate to their favorite charities and truly enjoy their lives.

Another of our clients demonstrates that even if you have waited until later in life financial happiness can still be had. You have time. Tired of living month-to-month, this guy made the decision to make saving a priority.

A hard working family man, he spent 20 years working around municipal workers, selling equipment to them, their districts and local government agencies. These employees had decent, guaranteed salaries and generous, publicly provided pension programs. Our client had nothing. Plus, at the end of the month there was too often more month than money; he never made enough to make it comfortably through the month for himself, his wife and two daughters. Typical of many working Americans, he was barely getting by paycheck to paycheck.

Then, in his mid-40s, he bought a heavy equipment dealership and began selling trucks to his customers. That allowed for a slightly better and steadier income. He used it to pay down his debt and help put his daughters through college. But the next thing he knew he was 52, and hadn't yet started saving for retirement.

Twelve years ago he became our client. We can still remember his wife, who worked with him in the business, writing the first check to begin their retirement account. Her hand was shaking out of trepidation. They still didn't fully understand how it would impact their lives. In the first year they saved and jointly contributed $25,000. They did that for each of the first three years.

As the business grew and their income went up, their lifestyle improved and they were able to put a little more away each year through the company profit sharing plan. Today, the husband and wife are in their mid-60s. They are able to fully retire and maintain their current lifestyle, which is considerably better than when he started the business. Now they don't have to work, although they still enjoy getting up each day and going to the office. Because of the financial decision they made to provide for their retirement, they work because they want to and not because they have to. Their future is set.

Additionally, their daughters are well on their own way to being set, too. Both joined the business after completing their educations. Even though they don't make that much money yet, they are already way ahead of most of their peers, having put away thousands of dollars each year. Also, they own their own homes. One daughter has a family with children and is now saving for the kids' college funds. Her goal is to pay for their education rather than take on debt to finance college.

Here is a family that suffered together for years before discovering the value of saving a little money as it went along. Today, parents and children are happy because they are confident enough has been done to financially provide for themselves. They no longer worry that there won't be enough money to make it through the month.

Yes, money can make you happy, but only from the perspective of what you actually need. People who make a lot of money often lose sight of what they need: Making it from the 1st to the 30th of each month. Many think because they earn so much it's no longer important to know what gets them from the beginning to the end of those 30 days.

If there's a gap between how much you make and how much you think you need to make, you'll never be happy. That's why it's so important to realize how much you really need.

It's funny how poor people and wealthy people face the same challenge. It's just that the numbers are bigger. Talk with an administrative assistant who doesn't own a home and has credit card debt and a modest car payment. She thinks she'll never get ahead financially. Talk with a wealthy business owner, a member of the stereotypical "1 percent," who believes his money problems are just as daunting as the secretary's. His credit card debt may be measured in the hundreds of thousands of dollars rather than the thousands. He may have a few million dollars in real estate mortgages and other loans. The nicer the lifestyle, the more expensive it gets. That's the only difference.

What distinguishes people who are financially happy from those who aren't, regardless of class or income, is their mentality. Without the right mentality, no matter how much money you make, it will never be enough.

No matter where we live, all of us know many people who are well off. "I'd love to change financial positions with that person." It's a common refrain. We've all said it at one time or another. If we only knew the complete story, we'd know that having larger numbers–of income or assets–doesn't necessarily make your life better.

Time magazine featured an important study by Princeton University's Nobel laureate economist Daniel Kahneman, who concluded that "money really can buy happiness–up to a very specific point." The research concluded that "money buys happiness for those earning up to around $75,000 a year." (This particular study determined that it isn't $50,000 a year that can bring happiness, as indicated by a study described earlier in this chapter, but rather $75,000). Earning more doesn't produce emotional satisfaction. "On average," the Time story said, "an American earning $575,000 isn't likely to be any happier than one making $75,000." Money allows people to have different experiences; it doesn't automatically allow them to be happier.

We see this reality playing out among the clients we counsel.

About eight years ago we had a client whose personal net worth was valued at more than $50 million. He lost everything. Today he is flat broke. Why? First, he didn't take our advice to protect a portion of what he had made during his "boom years." Primarily, he made bad business and financial decisions. He's not unlike the working class factory employee who once had net assets of a few hundred thousand dollars and who, when the recession hit, lost his house to foreclosure and his car to repossession because he became overextended and lost sight of planning and fulfilling his basic needs. It's just that our one-time multi-millionaire client did it on a much bigger scale.

At one time, our former client obviously profited from making good financial moves, and enjoying some luck, or he wouldn't have acquired $50 million. The only thing he never did was determine how to get from the 1st to the 30th of the month and figure out how to protect and preserve the assets required to do so. His psychological failure was never being satisfied with what he was making and thinking he would never have enough money. He always needed to reach for more instead of being content in the moment and protecting while preserving what he had, which was plenty.

How often do we see on television or read in newspaper stories about professional athletes, celebrities, big lottery winners or beneficiaries of large family inheritances who are blessed with lots of money--and seem to go through it at an alarming rate. They all share a common dilemma: They had their money before ever figuring out what to do with it. Many of them didn't have that problem prior to becoming rich; they knew then how much they had to spend each month and lived accordingly. Once they ran into good fortune, instead of maintaining their previous lifestyle and using the newfound wealth to improve upon it, they drew on the new money and outspent its ability to sustain their new and improved lifestyle. So they went from broke to rich to broke again. Most of the time serious tax and other financial problems followed.

The typical person assumes millionaires spend large sums of money on cars, houses and luxury goods--that they basically upsize everything in their lives once they come into money. Stanley and Danko belied those assumptions in their book *The Millionaire Next Door*. The authors determined the average millionaire has some common qualities. Most have cars that are about 10 years old. Most live in houses we would consider of more moderate means, not necessarily mansions. Most are people who don't value spending their money on extravagant entertainment; they typically enjoy spending time with friends and loved ones.

Millionaires studied by Stanley and Danko know that purchasing high-status items such as luxury cars or consumer goods that will depreciate with time are poor investments. They avoid the pitfall of "spending tomorrow's cash today," which results in accumulating debt, and is the main obstacle to increasing net worth.

Money doesn't cause or solve problems. It's just a resource like food or water. The decisions and perspectives about money are what shape your financial situation.

Another of our clients tells us money doesn't make him happy. What makes him happy is the stability offered by his job. He makes $60,000 a year. He earns enough to get by comfortably. He understands that the money he makes represents everything he needs to live on. This client is halfway to the right mentality. Now he just needs to plan, save and to be able to replace his income when it is no longer there.

There are two steps. First, realize how much it takes to be happy. Being happy is defined as meeting your monthly obligations with a little extra left over. Second, implement a plan to replace your income at some point in the future when it is no longer available. This can come either by your choice in deciding to retire or by a circumstance beyond your control, such as a disability or health issues or economic downturns.

The hurdle you create for yourself—what you need to live on comfortably—should not continue to rise with your income. If you're happy making $5,000 a month, your goal should be to replace that income when you are no longer working. The first goal in planning for your financial welfare should be to maintain your current lifestyle when you stop working. The only way to do that is to put a little money away over a long period of time. That way, when you stop working, your financial life as you have known it doesn't end.

Our message is that it's not as hard as you think. People procrastinate in putting away money for their future, not because it's truly difficult, but because they believe that it's difficult. The common belief is that by contributing into some kind of retirement program you are denying yourself something today. Instead, think of it as empowering yourself to achieve financial freedom and the ability to make choices in your life when the time comes.

Whether you will be able to work for the rest of your life is too frequently not a choice you get to make. If you have an employer, he can lay you off. If you're self-employed, health problems or the economic condition of your country, state or community can intervene. Don't be so self-absorbed as to think that just because you haven't done what's necessary to secure your financial future during your early years, you will have the luxury of working forever. It may not happen.

Young people often think of themselves as invincible. You don't imagine yourself getting old. When you're 28, 40 can appear so far away. But it feels really different when you're older. When you're 40, then 60 can seem a lot closer. Then you realize you should have done more when you were young.

We work at getting our clients to carefully calculate and then internally embrace an image of the magical amount of money they need to live on monthly. Then we ask them to imagine having that amount magically deposited into their bank accounts at the beginning of every month. Next, we ask them if they no longer needed to work–or couldn't work–would that monthly income make them happy. If it would, then we challenge them to create a plan for the future that provides them with that income– and we show them how that plan is achievable.

You don't need to make more money than you make today. The magical amount that ensures your future can be determined through a few calculations. However, until you identify that figure, all you will be doing in your financial existence is struggling, drowning and flailing about. There may be a lot of action and worrying, but very little progress towards accomplishing a realistic and definable goal.

When you change your perspective from trying to attain something you don't need—for example, I wish I had that rich guy's house, car and lifestyle—and focus instead on your own goals by determining what you need to last from the 1st to the 30th of the month, the burden becomes a lot less daunting. Then it isn't a burden at all. It becomes a goal that you can achieve.

CHAPTER TWO

You're Wealthier Than You Think *(Maybe)*

*"Money is only a tool. It will take you wherever
you wish, but it will not replace you as the driver."*

—Ayn Rand

FlexScore is a web-based financial scoring platform allowing you to literally score how well you are doing with your personal finances. It helps guide your decisions about saving and spending. It tells you what you should be doing differently. And it makes it all fun at the same time. We invented this solution for those who fret over their money dilemmas because we were tired of seeing people failing financially, even though they had the resources to really do quite well. This tool will help you make progress towards your own defined goals by awarding you with points for doing the right thing financially. It puts you in complete control of your finances and, because it is web-based, it provides you with constantly updated scores.

We offer a detailed, easy-to-understand explanation of what FlexScore is and how you can use it to achieve your goals in the next chapter. First, this chapter addresses what it takes to be financially secure.

It has nothing to do with the size of your bank account or how much money you earn. Like most people, you probably already have the raw materials with which to become financially independent. What most people lack is an understanding of how to use those resources and the tools already around them to shape their economic future. Put simply, it's about saving, not spending. FlexScore can help you do that.

We talk with our clients who are newly involved in the world of financial planning about the need to focus on the things they can control. We can't control the world or national economic climates or the consequences of the financial and housing meltdowns that spawned the Great Recession. However, we can control how we spend, how we save, and how we invest our funds. Frankly, it's not very exciting to talk about saving or investing, for the most part; spending is a lot more fun to talk about–and to do.

Let's examine this concept of people using the resources they have available now to set up their financial future. Where are these resources? Look around. The No. 1 resource most people possess is an income. It is a great resource.

Yet if people don't grab a hold of that resource or if they waste it, as many do, there will never be an opportunity for them to turn that resource into true wealth. It's as if you have been living on top of a vast store of oil for 25 years, knowing it is there but never actively drilling down into it. You have the resource. You just haven't understood how to actively leverage that resource and turn it into genuine wealth, a source of potential wealth that transcends the monthly wages or salaries you earn by working at your job. Look at it another way: If you're tired of living paycheck to paycheck, only you can make a change.

"Well, I don't make enough to be able to save for my future." We hear that excuse a lot. But after working during our careers with thousands of individual households, we've concluded that the overwhelming majority of them do have an income sufficient to ensure their financial future. There are only a relative handful of people we can remember whose real problem was not enough income instead of too much spending.

The American journalist, author and pop sociologist Vance

Packard wrote his classic book, *The Status Seekers*, in 1959. In it he argued that the difference between the working class and the middle class was the middle class' capacity to postpone gratification. Many of us are familiar with the experiment of placing a single marshmallow before each child in a classroom full of preschoolers. (It comes from a 1960s study of 4-year olds by scientists at Stanford University spearheaded by Walter Mischel, a psychologist.) "This is your marshmallow," you tell the children. "You can eat it now if you want. Or would you like to have two marshmallows? If you will wait 15 minutes before eating this marshmallow, I will give you a second marshmallow. But you won't get into trouble if you eat the first marshmallow in the next 15 minutes. Then you just won't get the second marshmallow. It's your choice." More than 10 years later, Mischel found in his experiment, the kids who waited for their second marshmallow did much better on the SAT than their peers who ate the first marshmallow straight away, bolstering the view that elements of what authorities call "emotional intelligence," such as controlling your impulses, are closely tied to students' academic achievement.

The lesson? If you use up more resources than you need because you want to satisfy life's immediate indulgences, you will never have an opportunity to save and use your resources to acquire other, more permanent things ("appreciative assets" in our parlance) that will grow and allow you to someday have more marshmallows without having to work for them anymore.

Too many people postpone confronting the pressing need to take action for their financial future, telling themselves they'll always be able to take care of their needs so long as they have the resource of an income. But what happens when you run out of resources, and income, because you don't want to work or you can no longer work? Do you just hope someone else will come to your aid? What if there are no more marshmallows to be had?

It is possible to look around and convince yourself that the grass is always greener over the next horizon, and that spending your money now will make you feel better. The immediate gratification of spending, which often derives from seeing other people you know doing it, justifies the practice. Satisfaction comes from the act of purchasing the trendiest consumer gadget or journeying to the hottest vacation destination, whatever is in vogue today. What people quickly forget is how long that instant gratification lasts and what happens after it goes away, when the bill becomes due.

For many of us it's a habit we pick up during early childhood. Remember when you were five or six during the weeks and sometimes the months leading up to the holiday season? You and your siblings and little friends got yourselves all worked up. You said to yourself and to each other, "It's going to be great!" You could barely wait with breathless anticipation and desire for the coming of Santa Claus and all those neat toys, presents and treats. And the only resource you needed to exchange for all of this largess was being a good boy or girl; sometimes parents let it slide even when you weren't all that good.

Then the great day came. You hit the peak of energy and excitement. You used and played with all of your new toys that day. But two or three days later do you remember how you felt? Was it something of a let down? Even if you got everything you wanted, it was different. You no longer had everything to look forward to. The excitement was over. You began to understand that even the best behavior wouldn't get you any more toys. And to top it off, you were going back to school the following week.

The only thing you didn't have to worry about as a little kid was paying the bill for all that just-passed excitement and happiness. That was your parents' worry.

Many people learn the lessons from these experiences once they grow up into adulthood and maybe become parents themselves. Some don't. As an adult you realize you don't need to be good in order to earn the goodies you desire. You don't even need to wait for one season out of the year. To enjoy your own Christmas whenever you want all you need to do is spend your own money or spend someone else's money that you borrow through credit cards or other forms of debt.

"Pleasure now is worth more to us than pleasure later," Northeastern University economist William Dickens recently told Newsweek magazine. "We much prefer current consumption to future consumption. It may even be wired into us." Scientists have found "measurable differences between the brains of people who save and those who spend with abandon, particularly in areas of the brain that predict consequences, process the sense of reward, spur motivation and control memory," Newsweek reported. Meanwhile, those who aren't very good at saving "are neither stupid nor irrational—but often simply don't accurately foresee the consequences of not saving," behavioral economists and psychologists have concluded.

It used to be that many people with limited resources had a limited ability to shop and buy. Once their dollars were gone, so were the opportunities to spend. Much of that reality went away, especially beginning in the 1980s, with the easy availability of credit card debt and home equity loans. In fact, access to debt became much more readily available for tens of millions of people. Even people's homes, which used to be seen as places where they lived, became leveraged as if they were personal ATM machines printing money. People refinanced their residences not necessarily to obtain a more favorable mortgage interest rate and lower monthly payments, but to also take money out of what for most people is their biggest asset in life. All this contributed to the housing bubble that eventually burst and to the spending addiction that continues to plague much of American society.

Ask yourself to identify the source of your own financial difficulties. Are you short on income or large on expenses? So many people spend as if they are wealthier than they really are. For many years, Americans have exhibited the "I'm as rich as they are" mentality. It's as if so many are unwilling to wait for the financial goal to be achieved before the reward is realized. As a society, we believe that debt for any and all purposes is okay. Go ahead and take that fancy trip to Europe. Just charge it and we'll figure out how to pay for it later; we'll pay for it tomorrow. We've all heard it before from others, and ourselves. But the truth is so true: Tomorrow often never comes.

How many times have we heard people remark with a sense of relief, "I just paid off that trip to Europe" three years after the big vacation? How many of us have said something like that ourselves? What many don't remember is that by putting the vacation on credit cards with high interest rates paid off over time, the trip that initially cost us $5,000 really ended up costing us $7,500 because of interest payments. We would never consciously pay 50 percent more than something was worth, would we? In reality, Americans do it all the time.

All of us have seen a friend, neighbor or family member drive up in a brand new luxury car. We think we know enough about that person to assume he or she probably can't afford the vehicle. (We may not know for sure that this person has more money than we do; we don't have the luxury of reviewing balance sheets or knowing the details of his or her personal finances. But we make assumptions.) Nevertheless, there it is, this beautiful new auto. And it's infectious; it gives us a want, too. It makes our three- or four-year old car look shabby by comparison, even though our car works perfectly well and gets us to where we need to go and back. Since we view this new car owner as our peer, or even as less financially successful than we are, we're convinced that we also need to step up our game and buy the same kind of new vehicle.

This is how addictions get fueled. You feel left out. "If this person has just bought that new car, then I should be able to do the same," you tell yourself.

It is so easy to convince yourself that spending that money will make you feel better and that you will always have enough time to make provisions for your own and your family's financial future. Practicing immediate gratification is made all the easier by the instantaneous coolness of this or that new consumer product, vacation destination or trendy gadget. Justifying this conduct by postponing what you know you need to do to create financial security comes from seeing other people you know doing the same thing all the time.

What you don't see is how long that instant gratification from the cool feeling lasts and what happens after it goes away and the bill comes due. Only, you're no longer a kid who can let your parents worry about paying for all the Christmas presents and goodies. Now paying the bill is *your* problem.

Spending, particularly with money you don't have by going into debt, can become as much of an addiction as being held hostage to alcoholism, drug abuse or gambling. Scientists have conducted research using functional magnetic resonance imaging (fMRI) machines to measure the brain activity of people when they are offered choices about whether or not to delay gratification. Researchers have firmly linked activity deep within the brain to subjects' decisions to delay gratification or not. (Remember that Newsweek report and the marshmallow research at Stanford? These people were among those tested in later decades with fMRI technology, which indicated that instant gratifiers and delayed gratifiers registered reactions in different portions of the brain.)

Even people who aren't plagued by psychological or physiological addictions to spending aren't protected from falling into a keeping-up-with-the-Joneses mentality. You see the neighbor's new car. You feel left out. You don't see any reason why that person has bought that car and you shouldn't be able to do it, too. We have friends with expensive watches. Why do we even need a watch in this era of computers and smart phones? But since my friend has one, so should I. And you tell that friend, "Nice watch."

As financial advisors, we have good friends who lost their homes because they fell victim to these kinds of impulses. One middle-class couple we know well had kids. They worked at good jobs and pulled down a good combined income, exceeding $120,000 a year. Yet over a period of years they took fancy vacations. They didn't just fly to Hawaii; they went to the most expensive resorts on the islands to swim with the dolphins, took private helicopter tours, ordered daily room service and took trips to the spa. They partied it up and had a great time on their vacations, along with the other consumer purchases they made. Then the burden of debt from financing their trips and buying their gadgets became too big for them to service. Before they knew it they were $100,000 in debt to credit card companies. Making minimum monthly payments sucked up an increasingly high percentage of their monthly budget. Their outgo was far greater than their intake. Even when this trend became apparent, their spending habits still far outpaced their monthly cash flow. When they lost their home, they chalked it up to the housing crisis and the bad economy. Sure, those were factors, but they weren't the primary cause of this couple's financial woes.

Ironically, even after this couple lost their home, some of our mutual friends who made similar incomes and faced similar financial circumstances looked at the lavish vacations and other spending behaviors that caused the predicament and probably said to themselves, "Why shouldn't I take those vacations and buy those things, too?"

Of the thousands of face-to-face planning meetings we've held with our clients over the years, both families and individuals, it is clear to us that the overwhelming majority of people don't have an income problem; they suffer from a spending problem. There is only a relative handful of clients we've counseled to either find better-paying jobs that would more appropriately compensate them or to seek a better education to improve their skills, if that was necessary to find more gainful employment.

Some of the happiest and most financially satisfied clients we've met with, often through advising them about their companies' 401(k) retirement plans, are blue-collar workers who don't make what we would consider a lot of money. They put in an honest day's work. They're happy to make it to Friday night when they can enjoy pizza and beer with family and friends. Their weekends are taken up with family outings or pursuing their favorite hobbies.

Jason's Uncle Lee worked for 42 years making wine bottles in the glass plant at the E&J Gallo winery, one of Modesto's biggest employers. He was good at his job. He was happy to have steady work, make a decent wage and enjoy a good retirement plan. He saved his money and invested in the company's retirement program. He liked having enough money at the end of the week to take the family out to dinner. All his needs were met. He just retired to a nicer lifestyle than he had when he was working. Why? Because he continually focused on the 1st to the 30th of the month. He didn't constantly try to trade up houses or cars and incur new and higher mortgage costs and car payments. He lives in the same house Jason visited when he was a kid and he's driven the same vehicle for years. He's still married to the same woman. Because of the financial opportunities he was presented, especially his savings, he was able to retire when he was ready to stop working.

In our practice, which includes advising many 401(k) plan contributors, we've had plenty of experience with people working in glass plants, agricultural processing and steel fabrication facilities, and home, commercial and pool construction. Everyone at these companies started out with the same opportunities and resources. Not all of them turned out like Jason's uncle, but those with foresight and discipline did. It would behoove many of our other clients who hail from professional backgrounds and benefit from much higher incomes to heed those lessons. The factory or construction workers earning $50,000 or $60,000 a year might wish they were white-collar professionals because they think making so much more money will make them happier. Ironically, so many of the white-collar professionals who make more money have supersized almost everything in their lives, and actually end up with dramatically fewer resources than the blue-collar workers who have saved and planned for retirement.

That doesn't make the blue-collar workers more virtuous. It's not that this class of workers has a greater ability to save. But it can go back to their different perspectives about money and providing for their futures. In a sense, most of the blue-collar workers aren't subject to quite the same cravings. A typical member of the working class knows that he can't afford a Mercedes-Benz, a fancy watch and a first-class flight to the vacation at the Four Seasons resort with five-star dining. Don't get us wrong: Those can be great experiences, but they won't necessarily make you happier.

You can enjoy almost the same sense of relaxation and satisfaction by getting away with your family to a vacation destination within your means. You can stretch out on the sands of a nice Hawaiian beach and gaze out at the same blue Pacific Ocean. While you're lying there, you don't have to be stressing out about how you're going to pay for it all. The stress comes from having to take on a burden of debt to pay for things you can't afford.

You have within you the ability and the power to change your spending habits and get out from underneath the burden of debt. Doing so will help relieve yourself of the tremendous stress that comes along with the burgeoning debt plaguing too many Americans. When you're an adult and have to pay the bills for that big fancy trip you couldn't afford, the stress lasts long after the excitement and relaxation from the trip have gone away. When the stress lasts longer than the fun, you know something is wrong. Living in the moment on someone else's dime can be enjoyable and spontaneous. Some may not think it is as much fun as saving to experience the moment later on when you have already paid for it. But saving for the trip and then going on it is more rewarding than going on the trip and then paying for it. It also makes more sense financially and emotionally.

Another affliction sometimes besets people's financial thinking. It's not unlike those who struggle to lose weight, succeed in shedding some pounds and then decide to reward themselves by going on an eating binge. People who see the light and maybe make some initial progress towards reducing debt or saving money can suddenly feel self-righteous; they feel entitled to a reward. So they say to themselves, "I've started putting some money into the retirement fund or paying off that older car; I'm going to go out and buy a new car as a reward." This kind of rationale doesn't work in either losing weight or paying off debt.

When it comes to deciding whether to take on debt for any reason, there are some operative question we need to ask ourselves: Can I live without that upgraded car? Can I continue on without indulging in that extravagant vacation undertaken on impulse? Can I make do without those expensive dinners followed by those front-row season tickets to the theater? Can I keep on going without that trip to Best Buy® where I'm coming home with the latest big flat-screen television and the powerful surround-sound system to go with it, when the old TV and speaker system work just fine?

You have to make a choice between instant gratification offering temporary pleasure on the one hand and financial security providing long-term satisfaction and peace of mind on the other. You can satisfy yourself today or secure your future tomorrow. The choice sometimes presents itself on a daily basis. It's a decision you have to make.

Too many people automatically choose the short-term over the long-term, not because they don't know any better but because they don't believe long-term financial security is achievable for them. One in four people think their best chance at achieving long-term financial security is winning the lottery. If you think that sounds far-fetched, check out these odds from the website Funny2.com featuring off-beat anecdotes, jokes and facts.

- Odds of winning Mega Millions: 176,000,000 to 1
- Odds of winning the PowerBall: 80,089,128 to 1
- Odds of being an astronaut: 13,200,000 to 1
- Odds of drowning in a bathtub: 685,000 to 1
- Odds of dating a supermodel: 88,000 to 1
- Odds of writing a New York Times best seller: 220 to 1
- Odds of becoming a pro athlete: 22,000 to 1
- Odds that the pilot of your airliner is a convicted drunk driver: 117 to 1
- Odds of bowling a 300 game: 11,500 to 1
- Odds of dying from a snake, bee or other venomous bite or sting: 100,000 to 1
- Odds of getting a royal flush in poker with the first five cards dealt: 649,740 to 1.
- Odds of winning an Academy Award: 11,500 to 1.
- Odds of being struck by lightning: 576,000 to 1
- Odds of actual death by lightning: 2,320,000 to 1
- Odds of being considered possessed by Satan: 7,000 to 1

In other words, don't count on the Lottery to be your retirement plan. You're 300 times more likely to be struck by lightning.

Getting started on the road to financial security can seem counterintuitive if you listen to Dave Ramsey, a well-known author, radio and television personality, and motivational speaker on financial matters. According to Ramsey, people who decide to start paying off their debt think they should start with the biggest item of debt sporting the highest interest rate. No, says Ramsey: Start with the smallest source of debt. He argues that managing your finances is "20 percent head knowledge and 80 percent behavior. You need some quick wins in order to stay pumped enough to get out of debt completely." So, by dispatching smaller, easier-to-pay off debt quickly, you will score immediate victories that snowball into further successes taking on larger debt burdens with higher interest payments. Doing this will encourage you to keep building momentum by moving forward to attack bigger debt reduction challenges. Ramsey calls the process his "Debt Snowball Plan."

No matter how you end up putting yourself on the road to debt reduction or savings, the central theme of this book is that if you make the decision to favor long-term over short-term gratification and make that decision real, it is very possible to achieve financial security.

The first decision you have to make is whether you are driven by wants or needs. Ask many people to give you their list of wants and 90 percent will immediately fire them off. Ask them to list their needs and the response will be much slower People aren't as in touch with their needs. What is that monthly nut you need to crack?

Chipmunks spend much of their waking hours foraging for the fruits, nuts and worms on which they survive. Once they acquire enough they stop foraging. Most human beings never stop foraging. They strive to make more money, build more resources and possess more things even when they've acquired enough to meet all their needs. Some basic needs are necessary to get through life such as food, shelter, clothing, education and transportation. Wants are things that are above and beyond needs. You don't need a steak dinner every night. You can survive on Top Ramen just as well even if it would be a boring diet. You don't need $200 designer jeans when a $25 or $30 pair of Wrangler Jeans is perfectly suitable. Wants are those things that make you salivate: The nicer car, the better shoes and the in-ground swimming pool. Everyone's wants are different. Unfortunately, the common denominator is that whatever people focus on, they just seem to want a nicer version of it.

We've been citing luxury goods. But a good example with which all of us can identify is the vacuum cleaner. Say the man of the house does the vacuuming, and he is really into it. He has a perfectly functional vacuum cleaner that works well. But he wants a Kirby or Rainbow model that can sell for well over $1,000. The new model would do the same job as the functional, lower-cost vacuum. Well, maybe the fancier one will be marginally better, but to what end? Both the existing and the more expensive vacuum cleaner will clean the carpets. So does the man of the house need the Kirby or Rainbow model? He probably doesn't. Does he want it? You bet.

What are those things in our lives that may not even be luxury goods but are still on our "wants" list because we want them? Or we scale down our wants, but we still desire them: "Honey, I'm not asking for a brand new set of golf clubs, just that great new driver I saw advertised in Golf Digest."

Not long ago a woman in her mid-60s came to us for financial guidance. She had already decided on a plan to retire, but wanted to know the best way to proceed. The first thing we noticed was she hadn't saved or invested enough to retire. Her goals in retirement were also far grander than her limited nest egg. When we explained this to the lady, she replied in a very matter of fact way, "That's okay, I'm going to retire anyway."

We explained the consequences of running out of money before she runs out of life. "That's okay," she said, "I probably won't live a long life anyway." She gave us additional background: Multiple marriages. Bad luck with men. Lots of stress as a result. "I fear my health won't last much longer," she offered.

"What do you mean? You think something will happen to your health?" we asked.

"No."

"Do have any illnesses or health problems now?"

"No."

"So as far as you know, you're just as healthy as when you were in your 40s?"

"Yeah."

"Then why have you decided to retire now when you don't have enough money to last over the rest of your life?"

"Because I feel now is the time I need to do it. And I've found a great deal on a house I want to buy."

"How will you fund the new house?"

"Using my 401(k) retirement account."

"We thought that's what you're going to use to live on in retirement."

"No, I'm going to use my pension," which she had in addition to her 401(k).

"Yes, but that's only going to cover 30 percent of what you will need to live on. How will you make up the difference?"

"I'm going to find a job."

"But you just told us you're going to retire."

It was a classic example of this I've-got-to-have-it-right-now mentality. She hadn't thought out her plans, "but it's what I'm going to do," she insisted. No person with a rational mind would make such disastrous financial decisions. But many people do because they haven't thought things through completely. This may be an extreme example, but at least this woman was more transparent in expressing her thinking, or lack of it. Her assumptions, attitudes and lack of consideration for her past decisions and financial future aren't that different than those held by many others who are aware of their wants but unaware of their needs. She epitomizes people whose lifestyles have far exceeded their needs. It is very common for them to be driven by impulse, whether it involves their buying habits or their fantasy plans for the future. Many are not even conscious of their lapses in judgment.

It's easier to spot those who buy extravagant goods they don't need and surround themselves with the accoutrements of luxury they can't afford. It is not as easy to spot others who will declare, "Oh, I'm not buying that designer Coach purse." Or "I'm not the kind of guy who buys that fancy boat I'll rarely use." When we meet with these people as clients to go over their monthly expenses they will very often vow, "I don't buy many fancy things and I don't see any easy ways to cut expenses to save money." Yet these very same people could well own too much of a house or too much of a car, taking on big mortgage or loan payments that confiscate $500 or $1,000 of additional monthly income for a bigger home or a more expensive vehicle they don't need. We witness that reality among our clients every day. They are usually moderate, rational, thoughtful and well-centered people in every other way. They are also frequently unaware of their habits or decisions that prevent them from making financial progress.

Who among us thinks money is easy to come by? None of us do. Almost everyone thinks they work hard for their money. But do we genuinely respect the money we make? If so, why do we choose to waste it?

We waste it by not having a realistic grasp of our bad financial habits. We also waste it because our time is limited; we don't have unlimited time on this earth or in our working lives. So why waste the money we work so hard to earn by paying more attention to our wants and less attention to our needs? If what we really want is a secure financial future, then why do we waste the money we make and our precious time by looking outside ourselves for our surface wants and immediate satisfactions instead of looking inside ourselves for our true needs? Before we salivate over what we want, we must first know what we need. Needs should come first, and then wants second and luxuries third.

Falling back on our marshmallow analogy, we ask what if all of your marshmallows were produced by your own marshmallow machine, a machine you created through years of planning and investing for retirement? Each year you put a little more of that machine together, part by part, until your machine is completed and it will make marshmallows on its own without you having to add any more parts or make it any larger than it is. Once you do retire, that machine will keep producing marshmallows and you will no longer have to worry about where they will come from.

Within our practice, we've come across many positive and instructive examples of people doing well by building their own marshmallow machine.

A couple with four children first came to us when they were in their mid-30s. They owned and ran a small family business for a dozen years, but they grew tired of working day after day and year after year with little or nothing to show for it except meeting a modest payroll covering their three employees and personal bills. The couple's net monthly income after taxes and business expenses ranged between $10,000 to $11,000. They couldn't figure out why they weren't getting ahead. As many small business owners know, working for yourself as opposed to working for someone else means trading the traditional eight-hour day in order to get your shot at the American Dream, which requires laboring 12 to 14 hours a day, but without overtime pay and a company retirement plan. Also, since you're self-employed you have to contribute both sides of Social Security.

"What do we need to be doing better?" they asked us.

"What is the dollar amount it takes for you to live from the 1st to the 30th of each month?" we asked them. They looked at each other.

"We have no idea," they answered.

"Well, and this is the truth," we said, "until you know that number we can't help you with any other number. Go home and figure it out. Get out your bank statements, your business income and expense records, your checkbook and your credit card statements for the last 12 months. Then determine what it takes for you to live from the 1st to the 30th of the month meeting all your needs, and then add in a little cushion." We supplied them with some work sheets to help them with their calculations and sent them on their way.

The couple returned 10 days later and reported it took $8,000 a month for them to live. Yet their business was able to pay them $10,000 to $11,000 a month. "You had the capacity to turn that income into wealth all those years," we told them. They were sitting across the table from us in our conference room. They looked at each other. They looked at us. You could see the lights going on in their heads. They expressed a sense of regret and shame that they hadn't been doing better for a long time. "We worked so hard for our money," they offered. "How could we have been wasting it for so long?"

"We all do it," we replied. "Until that light goes on, you can't help yourself. The good news is that the light has gone on, you both have plenty of time and, thanks to the success of the business you built, you have plenty of resources with which to do it."

The next step was working from their existing resources and starting to build and protect their future. We set up a retirement account into which they made monthly contributions of $1,500, which were also tax deductible. They obtained an adequate amount of life insurance and disability insurance so if one or both of them died, became ill or disabled, it would not completely disrupt their family situation. Next, they made an appointment with an attorney to help them draft an appropriate will and guardianship for their minor children. Finally, we set up a plan to pay down their home equity line of credit in 18 months as opposed to just paying the minimum amount due every month, which is what they had been doing for the last four years.

After accomplishing all of the above, their business really began to grow. They attributed it to doing the right things financially. Once fulfilling their monthly needs, they invested some of the extra money into improving their business, which produced extra income. This couple is well on its way to a bright financial future.

Now they even have the additional choice of putting some of their new resources into college funds for their children.

Another client was referred to us by his certified public accountant. He was a 42-year old physician in a lucrative medical specialty, married and with children. He had worked in his private practice for 10 years and was earning a substantial income. But he had amassed more than $500,000 in consumer debt outside his home mortgage in the form of credit card bills, home equity and auto loans, and lingering student debt. The doctor needed help because, despite his high income and the fact he worked hard and put in long hours, he couldn't see any way to climb out of his cycle of accumulating debt. He suffered restless nights because he struggled with the reality that the more money he made, the further he fell behind financially.

We quickly discovered the root of his problem. He had become accustomed and quite comfortable with the so-called doctor's lifestyle. This lifestyle consisted of the fancy house and car, the luxury vacations, the five-star dining, the expensive country club membership and the latest expensive gadgets and toys. But all this enjoyment came with a steep price: Continuously packing on debt.

At the conclusion of our introductory meeting, the physician informed us that in a week he and his wife were taking off on a two-week European trip to visit relatives. Excited about the vacation, he was looking forward to all the luxurious accommodations and grand activities they planned for the get-away. We discussed setting up a follow-up appointment when he returned. But first we ordered a copy of *The Millionaire Next Door*, the book by Thomas Stanley and William Danko, to be delivered to the doctor's home in time for him to take it with him to read during the long plane rides. The book synthesizes extensive research on the common qualities of American millionaires, who have very different spending habits from what the public assumes. We arranged to insert a card in the book from us. It read, "Doctor:

It was a pleasure meeting with you. We look forward to our next conversation. We hope you enjoy your trip to Europe, but thought it might help you prepare for our next meeting if you read this book."

When he came back from his vacation, the physician called us and said, "Every college student should be required to read that book. It was an eye-opener to me about my current lifestyle and really challenged me to think and act differently with my money." He was eager to get together to find out how he could turn his high income into real wealth.

We met again, helped the doctor understand how he was spending his resources and wasting his income, and the high risks he was taking with his existing retirement accounts. We showed him how he could be much smarter with his savings plan and how he could significantly reduce his debt. We also discussed how he didn't have to lead the stereotypical version of the doctor's lifestyle in order to be a successful doctor and still live well above the lifestyle of the average American. As we were meeting with him, you could see something was clicking; the light was going on upstairs.

By the end of our session, he developed his own three financial priorities, and embraced them: First, get out of debt. Second, dedicate a current income stream to replace his income once he was ready to retire. And third, avoid falling into the superficial habit of living a lifestyle that others thought he should be living rather than one that met his needs.

Our physician client spent the next decade conscientiously turning his commitments into practice. He retired 80 percent of his debt outside of the home mortgage. He's aggressively funded his accounts for the future and is well on his way to replacing his income with other revenue streams that will produce for him once he stops working. He continues to live well but has not allowed himself to fall back into the commonly accepted trap of the doctor's lifestyle. He feels much better about his life today.

The financial stress is gone. Now he only needs to be concerned about concentrating on developing his practice and spending quality time with his wife and children.

Another couple approached us in their late-50s shortly after the husband retired from working 30 years at a very secure job with a big utility company. He had a small pension that was enough to get the couple from the 1st to the 10th of the month based on satisfying their current needs. That still left the other 20 days of the month that the pension didn't cover. However, upon retirement, his employer also handed him a lump sum benefit of $200,000.

At first the couple was giddy with excitement. That was more money in one place and time than they had ever seen during their entire lives. They thought it would last forever and began spending like it would, far outpacing the modest lifestyle to which they had become accustomed when the husband was working. Two years later, they had gone through $50,000 of the $200,000 nest egg. After realizing that their lifetimes would exceed their funds, they approached us for advice.

First, we worked with our clients to determine how much it would take for them to make it from the 1st to the 30th of the month. We factored in his pension and future Social Security payments that wouldn't begin for a few more years, when he turned 62. We allowed room in the monthly budget for their idea of reasonable entertainment in retirement.

When together we finished designing a budget that would meet their needs, it only amounted to 50 percent of the spending that made them plow through the $50,000 so quickly. The couple was shocked to comprehend how wasteful they had become. They quickly recognized that the source of their problem was basing their newfound lifestyle on having this "pot of gold" on which they had finally laid their hands; only that lifestyle couldn't be sustained for very long.

We showed them how much money they were wasting every month. With our help, they adopted a spending "diet" that closely resembled what they had comfortably lived on for many years. It wasn't that they had to accept less of what made them happy before; they just needed to get back to it.

They came to us with $150,000, what was left of their lump sum retirement boon. Twelve years later, they still have the $150,000, upon which they still draw to help fulfill their needs from the 1st to the 30th of each month. They still live in the same house, still drive better-than-average cars, still have lots of fun and now they are reasonably confident about having enough money to sustain their lifestyle for as long as they both live.

Most people today see having $1 million in a retirement account as a lot of money. In fact, it really isn't. A middle class couple making a combined $75,000 a year needs to have $1 million in retirement funds invested in a moderate-risk portfolio plus their combined Social Security income in order to maintain a $75,000-a-year lifestyle when they retire at the age of 65. In other words, $1 million doesn't give you a license to spend lavishly. It does give you the ability to sustain your current lifestyle, and nothing more.

Yes, you can start drawing down on the $1 million principal remembering that one day life will pass and you will no longer need the money. But few people know when that will happen. Remember, one spouse spending several years in a long-term care facility can quickly deplete lots of money, even with assistance from Medicare.

Too many people are busy trading their time for dollars with little or no consideration for their financial future. Ask yourself: How much stress could you eliminate if you knew you were debt-free and had $25,000 saved up? Or how about being debt free with a savings of $250,000? Wouldn't you put those goals on the top of your wants list if you thought they were truly achievable?

It can be done and FlexScore can help you make it happen.

CHAPTER THREE

What is FlexScore, How Does It Work & How Do You Know Your Score?

"Financial advice for the rest of us."

—FlexScore

Over the years, we've worked as financial advisors to so many people who knew they should be doing better with their money but felt they couldn't control their financial futures They observed what was happening across the nation and around the world and saw stock market volatility, plummeting home and real estate values, and government decisions that added to public wariness and uncertainty.

Over it all hung the lingering concern many Americans felt over the threat of international terrorism and the economic uncertainty it could bring.

Facing multiple dilemmas, people didn't know where to begin or who to trust when it came to getting advice about handling their money. Many were put off as well by the confusing jargon of Wall Street favored by too many financial planners. These looming issues came to the table when we sat down with our clients to review their personal finances.

These are all legitimate subjects we should be discussing in the public square. They can come up during one-on-one exchanges between financial advisors and their clients too. But very few of these topics are things we can do anything meaningful to control. However, there is one thing we can do something about: We can bring the world of financial planning to common people in everyday language they can understand. And we can give these people the ability to objectively determine their own goals, help them prioritize these goals and show them how they can be realistically implemented. So many people fear they have lost control over one of the most important facets of their lives: Their personal financial affairs.

When we first meet with new clients they raise the same basic questions in one form or another: How am I doing financially? Am I saving enough? Am I taking too much risk with my investments? Am I spending too much? What can I be doing better?

There is no meaningful way for us to answer those questions without conducting a full-blown financial evaluation and completing a plan for each client. This can be a costly and time-consuming exercise depending on the complexity of the client's financial situation. So we created the concept of FlexScore to give everyday people direct access to the knowledge, motivation and results they seek, with or without the help of professional financial advisors. We believe FlexScore is an invaluable tool for both consumers and advisors. We aren't worried about precluding the need for advisors similar to us, as there will never be a shortage of people who need help with their finances. In fact, FlexScore was also conceived as an invaluable tool for financial service professionals because it creates a new standard by which our industry can objectively measure the financial health of its clients and set them on correct courses to financial health, only with the clients' full understanding and participation.

Once we believed we had fixed the central problem confronting our industry—helping the average consumer by making the language and concepts easy to comprehend—we had to overcome the challenge that financial planning isn't very much fun. It's hard work. It's boring. It can become laborious and overwhelming because it is a dynamic and constantly changing discipline. Laws and regulations change. Economic circumstances, both national and individual, change, sometimes radically. There are economic downturns. There are job losses and promotions. All of these things can significantly impact a person's financial status.

Our solution? "Gameify" financial planning. FlexScore turns financial planning into a game. We award points that reward people for doing the right thing based on the goals they set. We take away points for behaviors that detract from meeting their goals. In these ways we also make the process fun. That's part of the genius of FlexScore.

FlexScore isn't some hair-brained scheme the two of us dreamed up based on an arbitrary or subjective contrivance. It isn't a phony 10-step program devised by a self-appointed financial guru. We're just two guys who know from experience that when people begin and complete the long form method of conventional financial planning—following through with six steps based on sound and time-tested industry standards—they effectively accomplish their financial goals more often, more quickly and in a way that surprises them. The six steps in the financial planning process detailed by the Certified Financial Planner Board of Standards are: (1) Establishing and defining the client-planner relationship; (2) Gathering the clients' data and ascertaining their goals; (3) Analyzing and evaluating their financial status; (4) Developing and presenting to the client financial planning recommendations or alternatives; (5) Implementing those recommendations; and (6) Monitoring progress in meeting them.

Most people are afraid of the process until we sit down and go through the steps with them. They fret that it will make them confront longtime weaknesses, real or perceived, and worry that it will result in things being taken away: For example, the fun experienced while spending that extra money they shouldn't have been spending. Finally, it is a process they don't understand, a process that has always been foreign to them, and one that intimidates them. It's like having to sign up for that college course you know you have to take in order to graduate, but dread; you wait until the last minute to take it.

We needed to remove the mystery and intimidation surrounding financial planning while maintaining the fundamental integrity of the process. It is the process itself that brings results. There are no get-rich-quick schemes. The only choice is between making yourself financially secure or doing nothing and irrationally hoping for the best.

We've practiced the six steps in this process as financial planners for a combined 27 years. This is the same method employed by our responsible peers in the industry who practice the art and science of financial planning.

The following process is how we take our clients through the six steps in the long form method of financial planning (without using FlexScore).

First, we hold a discovery meeting. Our clients must prepare for the meeting by doing at least an hour of homework, collecting and organizing all of their financial data and information. Then we as advisors take approximately two hours to review the clients' financial resources and liabilities. We probe the clients about their financial goals. We get them to articulate those goals and embrace them as their own. Once the clients leave, we work to create solution steps that move them closer to their goals, help them shore up their biggest risks and get them on track to realizing what they see as their financial objectives.

Finally, we meet with the clients again for another 60 to 90 minutes to describe the solution steps we have established and get the clients to agree how best to implement them over the coming three to six months or longer, if necessary. The entire process is driven by the clients' goals and objectives, and by their motivation in carrying them out. As planners, we cannot do all the work.

Clients must take upon themselves an integral responsibility, as much or more than we assume as planners.

The initial costs of paying for this advice and our time as planners range widely from $1,000 to $3,500, depending on the complexity of the client's individual situation. This doesn't include potential accountant or attorney fees. The costs can be much higher if the clients are high-earning professionals or business owners. All this does is give clients the steps to follow from that point forward.

Subsequent implementation often costs just as much or more depending on how much help the client needs or wants. It is very common to conduct multiple follow-up meetings over time. There can be periodic or frequent phone conversations as we help clients navigate their end of the process and sometimes hold their hands while it's underway.

The progress towards financial health is similar to people's struggle to improve their physical health by going to the gym and changing their eating habits. We all know what is required in a generic sense. The hard part is breaking it down into manageable steps and being able to draw upon a professional, a financial advisor or a personal trainer who knows what he or she is doing. You can show up at the gym and work out on your own. Trainers aren't 100 percent necessary. But a personal trainer can save you a lot of wasted time and effort, help keep you on track and make necessary adjustments and corrections. It is the same thing with a financial planner.

FlexScore is a way to maintain the integrity of this proven financial planning process while translating that process into a language average people can understand and use on their own, on their own terms and in their own time with or without the physical involvement of a financial advisor. At the same time, FlexScore makes the process fun and fulfilling because you can see the progress you are making at every turn.

FlexScore can be just as effective as the long form of the

formal one-on-one financial planning process you would undertake in person with a financial advisor. It brings you the same tools and techniques that are the standards in everyday use mostly with wealthier clients. By implementing technology we developed, FlexScore brings those same high-level skills and tools to the average American.

There are roughly 315 million Americans today. If you believe the Occupy Movement, the interests of only one percent, or more than 3 million people who are wealthy, are being well served by the financial services industry. FlexScore is for the other 99 percent, the remaining 312 million Americans.

FlexScore is so revolutionary that we filed for a patent with the U.S. Patent and Trade Office, now pending, covering its algorithm, which is an advanced and highly sophisticated formula with the inputs changing the outputs in a dynamic manner. Like any formula, FlexScore can be determined using hard copy spreadsheets and hand calculations. But because there are so many inputs that are dynamically determining the outputs, computers and on-line access are the best means of determining your FlexScore.

FlexScore is a welcome alternative to the only three options that people face when trying to figure out the state of their financial existence: Go it alone, hire a financial advisor or simply bury their head in the sand. Unfortunately, most people opt for the latter option and become lost in the financial wilderness of ignorance, insecurity and uncertainty. FlexScore offers every person financial clarity. Instead of lecturing or browbeating, FlexScore is an entirely new financial product that empowers people to take more control over their own financial futures. It is not your daddy's financial advisor. It doesn't wear a suit and tie. It's never played the back nine at the country club or collected fine Scotch. It doesn't drive a BMW, smoke cigars or take martinis over lunch.

A lot of people mistrust anything Wall Street says or does. The big brokerage firms that epitomize Wall Street have been viewed as focusing on big profits, big trades and caring first and foremost about their stock value and second about furthering and protecting the interests of their clients.

Both of us worked for large Wall Street brokerage firms early in our careers. We were paid to represent the best interests of the firm to our clients, which is what we did. Today, as independent financial advisors, we no longer work for a large firm. We don't represent any one firm's best interests to our clients. In fact, what we do today is represent our clients' best interests to the financial services industry because we work for the clients and get paid by the clients.

A good example of how the industry is set up is seen in one of the most popular and well-known mutual funds in the world, the American Funds Growth Fund of America. It boasts 16 different versions of the exact same fund. These versions are known as share classes. Each share class owns the exact same stock holdings. The exact same managers run each of them. The only difference is the way the person representing the fund wants to get paid. The only reason there are 16 share classes is to give the financial advisors 16 different options on how they wish to be compensated for selling you the same product.

Left to their own devices, clients will choose one share class, presumably on the basis of which one they think costs them the least. However, so much complexity is built into the financial services industry that it's often very difficult for clients to know how to make the right decision. The financial industry thereby gives itself a reason for being.

Too many financial advisors use jargon that alienates average people. There is another big advantage offered by FlexScore: We take the Wall Street lingo out of the process. We don't dumb or water down the content. We just translate it into your language. Financial planning at its core is very simple: It requires you to clearly and objectively evaluate your own situation, decide on a course of action and then take action. Using very plain language,

FlexScore helps you know what you need to do and then supplies the order in which action should be taken to benefit you the most.

FlexScore encompasses everything you own, everything you owe and everything you are going to do with your money from this point forward, all based on the goals you set for yourself. It is a summation of past financial decisions that got you where you are today. FlexScore affirms that your financial circumstance is dynamic and that you should be the person controlling its fate. If you're not, then who is?

Now let's get into exactly what FlexScore is and how it works. FlexScore comprises a maximum of 1,000 points, divided into two 500-point parts. The first 500 points we refer to as "building your nest." You score points based on getting your financial house in order: Reducing your debt on the road to eliminating it, saving a good amount, diversifying your assets and protecting your income. "Funding your nest" is the other 500-point section. Each sub category in both parts is based on the industry study the Certified Financial Planner Board of Standards conducts every five years by surveying thousands of practicing CERTIFIED FINANCIAL PLANNER™ professionals about what their clients need help with the most. The study reflects changing economic factors; for instance, the most recent survey, released in July 2012, weighs the financial environment in the wake of the Great Recession and how it impacts financial planning and decision-making.

Here are breakdowns for the eight steps in the first part of FlexScore, building your nest.

Goal setting. This involves articulating your personal financial desires. Do you want to retire at a certain age or fund your retirement with a certain amount of money? Do you want to save up for a large purchase or event such as buying a new house or car or paying for your child's wedding? This is where you lay out the life you want to live and the future fun things in life you want to acquire. These goals are as unique as the people setting them.

Investments. This is where you list everything you own that you anticipate growing in value or producing an income stream in the future. They can be items such as stocks, bonds, mutual funds, real estate holdings, private businesses and more.

Debt optimization. Not all debt is bad debt. Having debt can be fine as long as you use it in an optimal way. Holding an appropriate home mortgage is good because of the tax advantages from writing off interest charges and the equity you build up. Acquiring student loan debt is good because it's about improving your education and investing in yourself, so long as you know how to hold it with low or deductible interest. Examples of bad debt include any credit card debt because it is, by definition, money you spent but didn't have to begin with; credit cards enable you to buy things you can't afford in the first place. Using credit cards to make purchases and paying off balances at the end of the month is perfectly fine; that's not credit card debt. Carrying forward balances on your cards is bad. So is that boat you bought and are still paying off that's sitting in your garage, the one you use only several times a year. Any other toy you buy—a recreational vehicle, that sixth television set for the house or a timeshare—is okay if you have the cash to afford it; it is terrible if you're using debt to buy it.

Protection planning. This encompasses everything you need to do to protect your income, property, your family and your nest egg from injury, destruction, illness, death and incapacity. So, for instance, it embraces life and disability insurance.

Retirement planning. The concept of retirement has changed. It used to be this vision of the Golden Years, when you hit a certain age, say 62 or 65, and just spend the rest of your life in carefree retirement. These days many younger people, those under 40, aspire to a time when they will no longer have to work as they presently do. They may look forward to turning 50, saying goodbye to the conventional corporate job and working 15 or 20 hours a week pursuing their passion while still drawing an income. Unfortunately, because of poor financial planning or bad economic winds many people who are between 40 and retirement age have concluded that retirement of any kind is unachievable for them.

It's important to remember one simple definition for retirement: When your financial resources and your mental desire to no longer have to work coincide. It has nothing to do with any given age. We have clients who tell us, "I'm going to retire at 60 years of age no matter what." They may have mentally prepared themselves for retirement at 60, but they have failed to be able to do so financially and maintain anything close to their current lifestyle. So the desire to retire and the ability to retire can be two completely different things. You need to be financially able to retire before you are mentally prepared or you're just kidding yourself.

Estate planning. Don't stop reading: Everyone needs to do estate planning. Why? If you're 28 years old, married with young kids, you need to tell someone who is responsible what will happen to your spouse and minor children in the event of your death. Estate planning gives instructions to those who will survive you when you're gone. You lay out what you want to happen to your assets and how you want your loved ones cared for.

Most people think estate planning is just for that rich couple already in their 60s. In fact, young people with children arguably have an even greater need for it. Is it probable something will happen to you at such a young age? No. Is it possible? Yes. Estate planning can be incredibly complex for people with complex financial situations. It can involve an intentionally defective grantors trust, a family limited partnership or a charitable remainder trust or an irrevocable life insurance trust. On the other end of the economic spectrum, for people of more modest means, oftentimes a simple will can suffice.

FlexScore helps determine the complexity of your individual situation and the appropriate estate planning steps that are necessary to ensure your goals, wants and desires are respected.

Tax planning. This involves trying to reduce the necessary evil of what we all have to pay the government consistent with existing tax law.

Cash flow. This is the art or science of making sure on a monthly basis you are not going backwards when it comes to your net worth by spending more than you make. It's guaranteeing you are heading in the right direction with all your available income sources. This means knowing how much it takes to get from the 1st to the 30th of the month, staying within those boundaries and knowing when you step outside them what the consequences will be in terms of distracting you from meeting the goals you have adopted. Cash flow is one of the least complex steps you can take towards financial health, but it is also one of the hardest for most people to master. You need to be focused on it at all times.

FlexScore is not a tool that will help you make more money. Instead, it will help you better use the money you already have in accomplishing your financial goals.

The final 500 points of FlexScore, funding the nest, are broken down into six sections.

Asset liquidity. This involves the liquidity or flexibility of your assets that will be used in the future to fund your monthly income. The goal is having assets that are easily available to generate income or available to be sold without negative tax consequences or holding periods. If all of the money providing you with an income is tied up in one investment, that may be terrific, but only if it's performing well. That asset could also be liquid, but it may not be flexible. If your money is tied up in complex financial products or real estate that could cause you to owe taxes or penalties or cause you to accept an unreasonably low sale price just to get your hands on some cash if you suddenly needed to sell them, then they aren't good examples of clean liquidity.

Asset diversification. Do you remember your mother warning you not to put all of your eggs in one basket? Asset diversification is the spreading out of your money, making sure you own a wide range of investments such as stocks, bonds, mutual funds and real estate plus other assets that may increase in value over time or hedge against the fluctuation in value of your other assets such as gold, oil and Treasury inflation-protected securities.

Debt to net worth ratio. This measures how well you have accumulated assets in relation to the amount of debt you owe. You will be rewarded for increasing your net worth when that increase occurs by either paying down debt or building up assets. The reverse will also be true: You will have points taken away when debt begins to rise more quickly than your assets.

Monthly housing cost ratio. This is about not spending more of your monthly income on housing than you can afford. This means living within your means whether you own or rent your residence. Do not allow what you spend on housing to become more than 28 percent of your monthly income. When you exceed that monthly housing cost ratio you limit your ability to apply a portion of the money you earn each month to other important defined goals.

Consumer debt ratio. Also make sure the non-mortgage debt you pay monthly does not exceed 20 percent of your monthly income. In calculating your consumer debt ratio, include all credit card and loan payments, and everything else except what you pay on your home mortgage.

Staying on pace to meet your goals. Making sure you are on pace to meet your goals is the single largest category of points you can earn in FlexScore. Are you creating enough financial wherewithal to realize the particular goals you have set for yourself? If your goal is retiring at age 60 with $5,000 in after-tax monthly income, you need to be putting away savings or earning money through investments at a certain rate each month between now and the date by which you hope to stop working. If your trajectory is on course or ahead of the pace, you will achieve your goal on time or even sooner and collect the full points allocated in this section. If you are not saving enough to meet that goal, your trajectory will fall short, and so will your points.

The financial life of a person or a family can be a complicated thing. There are mortgages, loans and other forms of debt, 401(k) plans, stock portfolios and life insurance policies, among many other factors. Most people find it challenging to properly assess all of these elements and figure out how they fit into the "big picture" of their financial lives. FlexScore provides an easy way for ordinary people to visualize and gauge their overall financial health.

Your FlexScore is based on a culmination of how you have done in the past and what you are doing currently, based on the points you earn in the categories we have detailed. You can see that your FlexScore is not based solely, or perhaps even substantially, upon how much money you make or how many things you possess. Rather, it is based on how you are doing on an array of interrelated financial facts about you and how you are or are not making progress in meeting goals you have selected.

A perfect FlexScore of 1,000 means you are ready. You've achieved all things in your financial life to meet your goals. Now it's your choice as to whether you want to continue to work. You can expand your goals if you like, or not. A perfect score allows you to live on more money, to have more fun or to maybe travel more or buy that better house.

Keep in mind that not everyone will be able to hit 1,000, even if they are diligent in their financial endeavors. Some goals may outweigh the capacity to achieve them. Many people don't realize how much savings are required to replace the working income on which they have relied. As mentioned earlier, to replace a $75,000-a-year income in retirement at the age of 62, you need to have around a $1 million nest egg, with about $40,000 coming from your nest egg and about $35,000 coming from the Social

Security payments of both spouses.

Some people think to themselves, "I can always draw down on the principle of my savings if it becomes necessary." Yes, that can be an option. But sometimes economic and real estate downturns on their own draw down principal or equity. Many retirement nest eggs lost more than a third of their value in 2008, when the stock and real estate markets plummeted. A hypothetical retiree with a $1 million nest egg would have been left with about $650,000 in asset after the 2008 economic downturn. So it isn't correct to assume you can always risk drawing down on the principal of your investments.

Another big risk people forget about is lasting longer than their money does, or running out of money before they run out of life. That is also the argument for saving more diligently when you're working, and monitoring your spending more closely in retirement.

Whatever your initial FlexScore number turns out to be, it will help you move far beyond just identifying your present financial position. More importantly, FlexScore will tell you how to improve it. It will give you the steps you should take to achieve your goals.

The true power of FlexScore is its ability to present you with clear, achievable action steps involving 14 quantifiable interrelated areas on which you can work to further your financial health. Like an MRI (magnetic resonance imaging) test that supplies physicians with a 360-degree view of the human body to further medical diagnosis and check on the process of disease and treatment, FlexScore is a new piece of technology that offers a 360-degree look at all things in your financial life; it focuses on them, continuously monitors them and supplies you with easy to follow steps so you can do better with your personal finances.

You may be strong or weak in any one or more of the 14 FlexScore categories. Because everything is ultimately related, strengths and weaknesses in one area can positively or negatively affect your scores in other sections. If your investments are doing really well when you're young, you may not have to save as much money later on. But if you are older, continue to take on or fail to reduce consumer debt and are behind in saving for retirement, you will see how it negatively affects your ability to realize the goals you have set.

Another major danger that can often be overlooked is how your goal can unravel outside of economic circumstances. Something may occur because of death, disability or the loss of a significant other on whom you rely. This is why life or disability insurance, or both, could be important in your situation; it is why we have included a protection-planning category in FlexScore.

What are your goals? Everyone's goals are unique. That's why your FlexScore is as unique as you are. FlexScore helps you manage both your short- and long-term goals while neglecting neither one. FlexScore helps make them happen whether you embrace buying a new home, saving for retirement, getting out of debt or a custom goal of your choice.

FlexScore doesn't set your goals. You do. FlexScore does help you identify the impact your goals have on your score, operating like a financial GPS. Knowing your FlexScore allows you to know whether your goals are reasonable and achievable or whether they need to be adjusted up or down. FlexScore isn't some financial advisor or self-described guru telling you what your goals should be and trying to impress you with how smart and knowledgeable he or she is. FlexScore requires that you determine goals for yourself based on the objective, realistic facts of your own financial circumstances that you have come to confront and understand, perhaps for the first time.

By helping you acquire and implement this knowledge on your own or by using it in consultation with a professional financial advisor, FlexScore brings industry standards to the masses of Americans who up until now have needed help but haven't been able to access it. In this way, FlexScore can also aid the professional financial advisor community. A key benefit from going through the FlexScore process is compelling you to flesh out all the financial issues and questions that are important to you. These are exactly the same facts a financial advisor would need to know about you during your first meeting. What are your goals? That's a question a financial advisor would pose to you. The advisor would ask you to detail what you own (a home, brokerage account, 401(k) investments) and what you owe (the debt you have taken on with other people's money). If the advisor is doing a good job, other key questions will arise such as "do you have proper protections in place such as life and disability policies, and adequate property casualty insurance such as auto and homeowner coverage?"

An advisor should also ask you whether you have provided for your intentions after your death. Do you have a will or trust? If there are young children, have you and your spouse talked about what would happen in the event both of you die? These are all inquiries a good financial advisor will pose. It's what we ask our clients when they first come to see us.

Once you have answered these questions and have embarked upon the FlexScore process, you are capable of executing the action steps FlexScore has established for you. Or you can decide to include the help of a financial advisor in the process. Then FlexScore gives both you and the advisor a big edge. It saves the advisor time and trouble, and saves you money because you've already done much of the advisor's work. In any case, FlexScore ensures a more accurate and precise result as you work with an advisor since you've already considered your most important financial issues. It's like the old adage, "garbage in, garbage out." If you go into the financial planning process already informed and knowledgeable, you will come out of the process with more thoughtful and beneficial advice.

When an individual middle class wage earner or salaried

employee seeks professional counseling about his or her $40,000 401(k) account, in most cases that person is not likely to find much interest within the financial advisor community. Some companies hire financial advisors like us to counsel their employees about their retirement investments. The modest individual investor is usually seen as "background noise" and even as a distraction for advisors who favor working with more wealthy clients.

FlexScore is clearly a benefit for the consumer. But it is also a tool that will make a big difference for the advisor community of which we are a part. Advisors working with their clients who use FlexScore will benefit from the thoroughness of its process and the fact it asks people to honestly look in the mirror and evaluate what's important to them about their money. It also asks people to decide what is more important: Reaching long-term goals or enjoying short-term satisfaction. Actually, FlexScore lets people do both in reasonable degrees: Enjoy some immediate satisfaction while they work to achieve much broader and longer-lasting goals.

Without the aid of FlexScore, talking to someone under the age of 40 about planning for retirement can be a difficult undertaking. People of that age think of retirement as something of concern to other people, meaning people with graying hair 20 or more years their senior. After all, so often people think of retirement as an age instead of an ability to no longer have to work, a time when your financial wherewithal meets your desire not to work. FlexScore helps people change the way they think about retirement and finances. At the same time, it gamifies the standards our industry uses to help consumers prepare earlier and better, which makes everyone better off.

In these ways, FlexScore is becoming the language of the financial neighborhood because of its simplicity, transparency and flexibility.

What keeps you up at night? What are those things you really want to do with your money, that you think you maybe should be doing but don't know how to get done? FlexScore gets that monkey off your back by showing you exactly what to do and how to do it. It isn't some abstract, theoretical exercise. It supplies concrete, simple and easy-to-understand action steps we know work because they're based on principles our industry has used to help people for many years. The hardest part is connecting your long-term future goals with the immediacy of what you need to do today to achieve momentum in the right direction.

How do you access and work with FlexScore?

FlexScore is a tool on the Web you can visit at home, from work, while shopping or eating. You can even access it from your mobile device. The formality of the financial planning process that people imagine, sitting down with a financial advisor in a mahogany-paneled conference room, is replaced by FlexScore. The reality is that you don't need the formality; you need the structure. FlexScore gives you the structure, but on your own terms.

The more you use FlexScore, the clearer your financial picture becomes, and the closer you get to reaching your goals. You can check on how well you are doing financially any time, anywhere. You can keep up to date through monthly emails that track your progress. You can learn how to reach your goals faster with free advice and customized action steps tailored just for you.

You can arrange to be notified as often or as infrequently as you like about changes in your score. You can receive reminders of the things you need to do to improve your score. FlexScore allows you to choose which action steps to conquer first. Steps that might take five or 10 minutes of your time and relatively little effort to complete could yield fewer points than those that take more time and greater effort. But those are decisions you make. What FlexScore does is let you see the direct correlation between your actions and overall financial improvement. Taking small actions will produce small improvements. Taking large actions will generate large improvements.

FlexScore will generate customized action steps for you to take. Acting on your steps will move you forward and improve your FlexScore. That FlexScore number will keep you continually engaged with your own financial life. As your number goes up, your life gets better.

If you have some money available each month, FlexScore shows you whether it's better to use it to pay off debt or to sock it away for the future. Because FlexScore presents a holistic view of your finances, it shows you which choice will do more for you at any given time. More significantly, the choices you make are based on the goals you set given your particular financial situation.

For example, if the goal of paying off debt is more important to you than retiring at a relatively early age, then FlexScore may recommend for now that a larger chunk of your free cash flow goes into debt reduction rather than growing a retirement account. If paying off debt is not a big priority but you have high debt costs in the range of 15 percent or higher annual percentage rates on credit card obligations and you don't like to take risks with your investments, FlexScore would probably also initially encourage you to pay off debt instead of putting a lot of money towards retirement. That's because investing money in lower-risk investments would likely yield a return rate of about 4 to 6 percent over the long term. The interest you're paying on those credit cards could be three or more times what you're earning from the low-risk investments. Therefore, the best use of your money would likely be eliminating those high interest charges by paying off the debt before working to build up a nest egg. Building up the nest egg is still important. But first you need to dig yourself out of the debt hole and get back to even.

This is not to say you have to pay off debt first or that you have to plow all your resources into paying off your credit cards or that you can't simultaneously take advantage of your company retirement plan if you have one. Participating in the retirement plan may present advantages, especially if your employer matches your investment; plus it's money that isn't now subject to income taxes.

FlexScore takes into account all of these considerations. It keeps your focus on those aspects of your financial life you *can* control: How much money should you put away each month? How much debt should you pay down? How should you invest your money? How should you protect your loved ones?

Finally, FlexScore is not vague, incomprehensible analysis. It isn't some insurance agent overselling you on insurance products for his benefit and not yours. It is not a stockbroker making a big commission each time your money moves around. It is not a confusing, overpriced financial advisor repeating the same mantra, "Just stay the course and everything will be fine in the long run." (What if you aren't even on the right course in the first place? Wouldn't that be a good thing to know now?) FlexScore is not a static picture of your net worth without accompanying advice on how to do better.

FlexScore is straight talking, Wall Street-lingo-free financial advice. It's your friend and trusted companion. We've deconstructed the old-fashioned financial advice model and reconstructed it with you in mind. It's comprehensive, simple, understandable, accessible and, dare we say, fun.

FlexScore is your financial life as you understand it and as you want it to be. Are you ready? Your score awaits you.

CHAPTER FOUR

Everyone's FlexScore is Different

*"Today you are you, that is truer than true. There is no one
alive Youer than You."*

—Dr. Seuss, writer of children's books

In an ideal world, we would all start saving and investing
for our future the day we land our first job. But as we all know,
ideal worlds usually exist in the realm of fairy tales. The real
world is a place filled with many challenges and hurdles we must
overcome. While there are many things we can learn about life
growing up, how to handle our own finances is not always one of
them. Reading, writing and arithmetic are all necessary subjects.
So are civics, history and science as well as a plethora of other
topics. Yet somehow along the way, the world of formal education
has committed a serious error in leaving personal finance off the
course schedule.

So let's begin the discussion with an unfortunate but true fact:
Learning about money usually doesn't occur in the classroom.
The consequences of this omission and its effect on our daily
lives are very real, as revealed in a 2012 study, an analysis of the
existing literature coauthored by William Gale, an economist at
the Brookings Institution and director of the Retirement Security
Project. He begins with consumer research showing 21 percent
of survey respondents thought winning the lottery was "the most

practical strategy for accumulating several hundred thousand dollars" for retirement and 16 percent believed a lottery bonanza was the best way all Americans will be able to retire.

Such "ill-advised financial decisions about retirement," Gale's findings suggest, also apply to the many people who do save but invest excessive amounts of their 401(k) portfolios in their own company stock or deplete their retirement accounts before they retire. It's a bad idea to unreasonably take out loans against retirement accounts, withdraw money during times of hardship or use the funds to satisfy immediate needs. Retirement accounts are for just that purpose: Providing income for your retirement.

Gale defines financial literacy as "the ability to make informed judgments and effective decisions regarding the use and management of money and wealth, as well as the ability and discipline to implement intended or desired saving behavior." The woeful lack of such literacy is well documented and the link between this inadequacy and common financial miscues are conclusive. Households peopled by the financially illiterate are less likely to save for retirement, invest in stocks, keep an emergency fund or even possess a checking account. They are more likely to patronize payday loan shops, accept costly mortgages, pay only the minimum required monthly credit card amounts, take on higher debt and fall behind in paying off that debt. All of these behaviors are milestones on the path to financial insecurity.

People with little or no education on personal finance, regardless of social or economic class, tend to rack up a ton of debt. They have little ability to retire that debt. And they have little or no ability to accumulate assets or investments over time to provide for their financial security. They continually dig themselves into financial holes, are constantly struggling to catch up and end up becoming beholden to other people if they are lucky. In other words, financial illiteracy can seriously impede the ability to have something to show for all the hard work people put in over the course of their working lives.

Recent changes in financial education are aimed at altering the status quo. Some 20 states are requiring that financial education be included in an existing high school subject's curriculum; four states demand students actually take an independent course on personal finances. Financial education is also being targeted towards workers at job sites, especially in light of the trend by employers who are using defined contribution offerings such as 401(k) plans in place of defined benefit retirement plans such as company-provided pensions. This means individual workers must take more personal responsibility for planning for their own retirement. (We are frequently brought in by employers to counsel their employees on the optimum use of their firms' 401(k) accounts.)

Both workers and students need to learn about the truly important financial factors that will determine their success in work and life. Sure, you have to be able to read and write. A certain proficiency in math, science and computer technology is also very important to function in today's world. Proficiency tests that are used to gauge student achievement and now determine whether they graduate from high school are based on measuring progress in these subjects. They are also increasingly the criteria used to judge whether teachers, administrators and schools are doing a good job because they are closely tied to youngsters' capacity to succeed in life. Then why do we still leave out personal finance even though it has such a direct correlation with our future success?

Excelling at reading, writing and arithmetic might allow someone to do well financially, that is earn a high income. But so many people fail to accomplish anything constructive with that high income. We have already provided examples of doctors and other successful professionals who pull down a high income and proceed through life assuming that alone will make them okay financially. Yet as we've demonstrated, having a high income and doing well financially are two separate matters. It's admirable when our schools prepare us to make a good living. It's a shame they don't prepare us to handle that good living. When it comes to personal finances, we are too often left to our own devices.

Parents frequently end up performing the lead teaching role in financial literacy. But many parents are just as unprepared as their middle or high school offspring when it comes to imparting this knowledge. Some families make a priority out of teaching their children the ins and outs of how to handle personal finances. But if you're like most people, your parents may not have taken the time to help you become savvy with money. The only education upon which many fathers and mothers can draw is their own history and experiences, which oftentimes haven't led them in the right direction. After all, if parents don't know how to handle money, it's not likely they will pass on many good habits to the next generation.

Most people lack a formal or informal education in personal finance. FlexScore helps to remedy this sorry state of education. We've developed a system that not only teaches you what to do, but also what not to do, all by using a simple point system. FlexScore is a measurement that encompasses all your good or bad past financial decisions and your current resources, connects them to the goals you have laid out for yourself and makes the whole process fun. As noted in the previous chapter, FlexScore's scoring system ranges from 0 to 1,000, with the score of 1,000 representing a user who has completely funded his or her goals, protected them from all known risks and accumulated assets that will produce enough money so the person can choose to no longer work for a living.

Not everyone is going to earn a score of 1,000. Sure, that would be nice, but many people find themselves contemplating retirement later in life or when they are on the brink of retiring with neither the time nor resources to fund their future and realize or protect all of their goals. Not all is lost. Making the decision to retire, even though your FlexScore may be in the 800 range, is still possible. The reason FlexScore is so valuable is because it is the direct representation of your financial decision-making.

Your choices end up taking you down a certain financial path. If you're not making informed choices, if you just make what-feels-good-today kind of choices, then you might end up finding yourself with a desire to retire but without the ability to do so. Determining your FlexScore number and keeping it in front of you on a regular basis maintains the top-of-mind awareness necessary to achieve any goal, especially a financial one. Having that FlexScore number staring you in the face means at the very least you will hopefully be making an informed choice about when, and under what circumstances, you will decide to stop working. Your score may not yet be 1,000, but at least you will know where you stand with no surprises, and you can make informed decisions accordingly.

Each person's FlexScore is as unique as they are. Let's take two different people, call them Sarah and Jennifer, working at the same company. Each is 45 years old and earning $75,000 a year. They both live in Colorado Springs, Colorado and aim to retire in 15 years.

Sarah is happy living in Colorado Springs, and plans to retire there too. Jennifer wants to move to Aspen, Colorado after she retires. Aspen is a town known to have a much higher cost of living than most communities. While both Sarah and Jennifer have saved the same amounts to date, use the same investment strategies and spend roughly the same amount of money to live monthly, Jennifer's FlexScore will inevitably be lower than Sarah's. How can that be if their current financial pictures are essentially equal? It's very simple. It is because Jennifer's retirement goal, living in the more pricy Aspen, calls for her having to save a lot more money than what she is on track to accumulate. In order to retire to Aspen, Jennifer needs to make different financial decisions today in order to meet her goal; she needs to put away a great deal more money than Sarah. Maybe Jennifer will take on a second job to save more. She might even press her luck and try to expand the return on her savings by making more risky investments. Just setting goals without consideration for the amount and trajectory of your resources isn't enough to be called financial planning. Everything counts. That's why FlexScore is so comprehensive; it counts everything, and in Jennifer's case that includes her goal.

So if one of your primary goals is living in a place such as Aspen, achieving that goal will mean taking in more money now. It could require you to go back to school to advance your job skills, angle for promotions or take on more work. If you're married and your spouse isn't working, it may mean your spouse will have to take on a job to produce more family income. Or it might mean you will have to work until later in life. Or you might have to pare down your vision of retirement; instead of that 2,500 square foot home in Aspen, you settle for an 1,800 square foot house. It will be smaller and cost significantly less, but you'll still be living in Aspen. FlexScore either sends a message that your current behavior needs to change (such as the need to put aside more money) or your goals for the future need to be adjusted (such as considering a delayed retirement or a reduction in retirement lifestyle) to accommodate your ability to fulfill them.

Jason's goal is to have a vacation beach house in the beautiful seaside city of Monterey, California. But his dream home is out of reach at the moment. His mind is still set on a house on prestigious Del Monte Beach in Monterey, which is second only in status to nearby Carmel-by-the-Sea. But Jason, being a seasoned financial planner, understands that goal is not attainable in the short term. So in the meantime, he is satisfied owning a home in an adjacent Monterey County community called Seaside. It's more of a working-class neighborhood near the new California State University, Monterey Bay campus with decent but more modest residences literally five minutes from Del Monte Beach. Jason's home looks out on the same blue Pacific Ocean you would see if you owned a home on Del Monte Beach, but it is one-tenth of the cost.

By settling for a house in Seaside, Jason still resides in the general vicinity he desires. It's not necessarily at the level he ultimately seeks, but he's there. Accepting that reality means Jason is able to make progress in reaching his other important financial goals. He is fully funding his retirement plan every year. He is paying down his home mortgage debt and he is saving to help pay for the college education of his three young daughters. In the tradition of the mid-20th Century sociologist Vance Packard, discussed in Chapter Two, Jason understands delayed gratification is important to reach his long-term goals, but it doesn't necessarily mean he has to deprive himself of any gratification; he's still fulfilling his dreams today by owning the home in Seaside. As a result, Jason's FlexScore is well on its way.

Can you have a higher FlexScore than Bill Gates? Yes, you can. Remember, assets and income aren't everything, even for the wealthiest man in America, who has assets of $66 billion. Assuming you are on the right savings path, have positioned yourself with little or no debt, are surrounding yourself with assets that appreciate or grow in value and have protected your finances from death, disability, lawsuits and unnecessary taxes, your FlexScore might be better than that registered by Mr. Gates. Yes, he is worth a bazillion dollars. But what if he hasn't appropriately guarded his wealth? What if he carries high risks that are not protected? If you've done everything you're supposed to do financially, then it is possible to have a higher FlexScore than someone who is renowned bazillionaire.

Assets are only one piece of the equation. The other 13 scoring criteria in FlexScore are just as important as accumulation of assets. Remember, FlexScore is based on 14 unique and interrelated parts. Just because someone succeeds at building assets doesn't mean all the other important financial requirements of financial life have been met.

Merely owning plenty of lumber, nails and hammers doesn't necessarily mean you can build a house. You also need the skills to put the lumber together in something that resembles a frame and then build upon it. But before you place your family inside that house, don't you first want to make sure the building is structurally sound? It's the same thing with people who possess substantial amounts of assets or are blessed with high incomes. They shouldn't rest on their laurels by believing they've already done well financially. Without appropriate steps to protect those assets, all they have accrued can someday come crashing down like a house that has been improperly built. We've seen it happen too many times.

Let's examine three different people at three different stages in their lives but all with the same FlexScore. These are just a few examples based on clients with whom we have worked over many years.

Alex is 31 years old, married and with two young children. He makes $60,000 annually.

Christine is 43 years old, divorced and with one child. She earns $85,000 a year.

Maria is 58 years old, married and with grown children. She takes in $70,000 each year.

All three of them have the same FlexScore: 650 points out of a maximum score of 1,000.

For Alex, 650 is a great score. He has begun a robust savings plan, putting away 10 percent of his annual income, and investing that money for growth and appreciation. He has no credit card or student debt. He has an affordable mortgage on his house. He and his wife also have written a simple will and have had it notarized. Because he has a young family and a wife who stays home with the children, Alex has protected them with life and disability insurance. (You don't think disability insurance is necessary? It won't happen to you? According to the Council for Disability Awareness, more than one in four of today's 20 year-olds will become disabled before they reach retirement. Roughly 12 percent of the total population, or more than 36 million Americans, are classified as disabled, and more than 50 percent of them are in their working years, between the ages of 18 and 64. There were more than 2.5 million disabled U.S. workers in their 20s, 30s and 40s receiving Social Security Disability benefits as of 2010.)

Christine is doing slightly above average, for now, with her FlexScore of 650. After her divorce, she was awarded half of her ex-husband's retirement accounts. But she has been unable to find a way to save more than 5 percent of her annual salary. The alimony and child support payments she receives provide more than enough income on which to live, but neither will last forever. She has a small amount of credit card debt, but nothing overwhelming. Christine is currently stagnating with a FlexScore of 650, but has the potential to do better. In fact, without a few changes in her financial affairs, she is in danger of falling below average.

Maria spent a great deal of her time and effort tending to the needs of her three children while they were young, and even when they were grown. She decided to pay for all of her kids' college expenses. After finishing college, her children needed more financial help. She gave it to them. Only recently did the last of her kids leave the house at the age of 28. Unfortunately, at 58, Maria has saved only about half of what she needs for retirement. When she was in her 30s, Maria always talked about retiring at age 60. She blames a lackluster stock market and her "underwater" home mortgage as reasons why she can't retire in two years. Sadly, neither of those things are the problem. Maria's chances of retiring within five to seven years at the same lifestyle to which she is accustomed are very slim. In her specific situation, Maria's FlexScore of 650 is below average. Her best prospects are for Maria and her husband to commit to a healthy savings plan and work longer than they had anticipated.

Further examples are offered later in the book.

CHAPTER FIVE

Financial Independence is For Everyone

"There's more time than life."

—Mexican proverb

Ultimately, no matter who you are, almost everyone has in common one financial goal, which is to become financially independent. Even if you can't achieve it now, you can work to do so at some point in your life. FlexScore is the vehicle to help you.

The average American views the term financial independence as something only for rich people. Many of them also find the word "retirement" a foreign notion. The answer to these dilemmas is to not allow yourself to become focused and hung up on the age or date at which you hope to retire. Instead, focus your energies on those activities that will allow you to stop working or slow down at some point in the future when you choose, when you are ready, when you are prepared and when you have created enough assets to replace your income so you no longer have to work. This doesn't mean you have to retire or completely stop working at that time. Then it becomes a choice, your choice. Sometimes it doesn't end up being your choice at all; you may have to end your career because of health concerns. How many people have we known who are in their 50s or 60s and were forced out of their jobs before they were financially ready because of illness or injury? That unfortunate exigency is all the more reason why you need to start preparing now.

As we've noted before, there is a genuine difference between being mentally ready and financially prepared for retirement. Traditional retirement occurs when two factors converge: mental preparedness and financial preparedness. Most people admit, at least to themselves, that they are mentally prepared to stop working well before they reach the traditional retirement age. Too often the financial side of things need to catch up. On the other hand, we also know people in our lives who are clearly financially prepared to retire but aren't yet ready for it mentally. They still have contributions they want to make during the span of their careers or projects to aid society they wish to undertake after they stop working.

One of the purposes of FlexScore is to help people transcend the traditional concept of retirement and adopt the more modern ideal of achieving true financial independence at any age. Then, if your mental desire is to continue working, so be it. At least you have the choice of no longer having to work. FlexScore will help take you to that place.

In this chapter we discuss some of the fundamentals of personal financial success. Many of them appear to be obvious on the surface because they are actions we simply need to take. Yet due to ingrained behaviors we've acquired and become accustomed to, often over a lifetime, the truly difficult part is not understanding we need to take these steps; it's in the execution.

Here in a nutshell are the basic tenets of financial independence based on standards long observed and practiced by professionals in the financial planning trade.

Set for yourself measurable and reasonable (realistic) goals. This means dreaming a little bit, but not so much that you can't attain what is truly within your reach. For example, saying that you want to become rich is not generally attainable. As we've pointed out, most people define rich as what other people have attained; they rarely know what it might mean for themselves. We've also mentioned that the hurdle continues to be raised each time you reach what you define as a worthy goal of financial success. In other words, the grass is perpetually greener on the other side.

The proper way to define a goal is to describe it in objective terms that can be measured and achieved given the average performance of both your financial behavior and the financial markets in which you play. You don't want to become the most fastidious cheapskate pauper who ever existed on earth. Most people can't and don't want to become that person. If you try to emulate the actions of such a person, you will inevitably fail. When some people envision radically improving their financial capabilities, they may adopt views of the performance of financial markets that are surely unrealistic. If your goal of retiring is based on achieving a rate of return on your investments of 20 percent a year, you will be quickly disappointed when you cannot repeatedly depend on this sort of utopian expectation.

A close friend of ours went to a financial advisor when he was 22. "If I put away $1000 a month, how long would it take for me to become a millionaire given a 15 percent annual rate of return on investments?" he asked. At the time, during the mid-1990s, this young man was only making $28,000 a year. A 15 percent return rate didn't seem such an unreasonable assumption because everyone else was scoring at least that much given the booming state of the stock market.

This guy's plan didn't work out because the idea that someone of his age and income was going to be able to invest $1,000 a month was totally unrealistic. He had just bought a house. He was putting his wife through college. He did benefit from holding no debt, including credit card payments, other than a home mortgage. The couple owned their cars free and clear. They were paying for the wife's college expenses out of monthly cash flow at a time when the costs of attending a state university were still reasonable. Yet freeing up $1,000 a month was still an incredibly impractical expectation. In fact, it never came close to happening.

Still, this young man was ambitious and disciplined. By the time he was 40, he accomplished his goal of becoming a millionaire. But it wasn't by putting $1,000 away each month beginning at the age of 22. It was because he and his wife discovered the tenets outlined in this chapter and followed them.

It is possible to realize your financial goals in a reasonable period of time if you possess the right attitude about money and what it can do for you.

All of us have heard stories about millionaires who went from rags to riches, lost it all and then came back stronger and quicker and even wealthier. Why is that? Is it luck? Or is it because they were passionate about their goals, realistic in attaining them and able to correct their past behaviors in order to march more quickly towards reaching their objectives? Actually, our friend from the above example did go from rags to riches to rags and to riches again in a relatively short period of time. He's still a few years short of middle age. But he knows if events outside his control cause him to lose everything again, he has the capacity to once more build up his wealth.

If our goal is to pay off $50,000 in credit card debt in one year and we only make $75,000 a year, the behaviors we would need to adopt to achieve that goal are so traumatic that we will inevitably fall short and feel defeated to the point where we will hesitate to set *any* goals, no matter how attainable they may be. When it comes to the type of goals we should adopt, an old acronym is worthwhile to remember: SMART. It stands for specific, measurable, attainable, relevant and time-bound. Let's take a closer look at those words, one at a time.

Specific. So many children growing up in America are convinced that life would be so great if only they were rich. But how does anyone define what is rich, regardless of whether or not this precept is legitimate? To fulfill this naive desire, the goal needs to be specific: A particular amount of cash in an account; a desired level of monthly income; or certain kind of home in a distinct neighborhood. Goals cannot be fashioned using generic or relative terms.

Measurable. Once you set course on your goal, you need to be able to reflect back and evaluate whether or not you're making adequate progress in reaching it. Let's say, for instance, that I set the goal for myself of quitting work at the age of 60. If I was 45 when that goal was laid out and it I haven't measured my progress in financially achieving it and now I'm 50, then retiring at 60 is a great idea, but it's just that: an idea. The only thing that changed is I'm five years closer to the age when I decided to quit work. The proper measure was what I was doing in the last five years to financially prepare for meeting that goal.

Attainable. Can your goal be achieved using the resources that are available to you now such as your income and access to financial products, your motivation in getting to the goal plus the knowledge and discipline required to reach it? Personal discipline is ultimately the most important key to success. You can earn all the money in the world, but if you're not properly focused, it can go as quickly as it comes.

Relevant. You can be passionate about and committed to getting something done, but your goal can be too nebulous. Don't just say, "I want to have a vacation home somewhere." Set the goal of buying a 2,000 square foot cabin on the lake at Pinecrest in the Sierra Nevada Mountains of California. This particular example may not be your cup of tea, but if you do set a goal, it needs to relate to what you are passionate about, what your dream is about and what you can remain committed to and focused on through thick and thin.

Time-bound. You know the actions you have set out will bring you closer to reaching your goals, but only by understanding that all of us have a limited amount of time remaining in our working years and, more broadly, on this earth. Unless a goal is grounded in a time horizon, every good-intentioned person will fall back on the age-old excuse, "I'll put that off until tomorrow." Tomorrow doesn't become a risk if our goals are time-bound and we create a greater sense of immediacy that pushes us forward to take action towards attaining them.

If my goal is losing 20 pounds in six months I can continue eating the way I've been eating for the next three months. But doing so really makes it all the more difficult during the final three months of my time horizon if I'm to have any chance of meeting the goal. A hard deadline helps you actually achieve the goal by continually focusing actions on the here and now rather than I'll-get-it-done later. Making goals time-bound constantly pushes you to take action sooner than later.

The next tenet of financial independence is knowing what you already own and owe. Not everyone does. Many people don't. Most people have a generic idea of what they have in their 401(k) fund, savings or investment accounts. But they may not know what sorts of investments make up the total value of their plans or accounts. People may understand at a certain level that they have taken on too much debt, but don't know exactly how much they do have and, more importantly, how much that debt is costing them every month in interest payments.

Many typical Americans are hard-pressed to accurately answer these questions: What was the rate of return on my investment or retirement portfolios over the last 12 months? How about over the last three years?

It's important to know the answers. What if you have set your goal of achieving, say, an eight percent investment return over the last 12 months or three years and your investments have lost money or have otherwise grossly underperformed? You need to determine whether you selected bad investments or whether you only suffered through the inevitable malaise that happens during normal economic cycles. If it is the former, changes would probably be recommended. If it's the latter, you may not need to do anything at all except consider saving more to help offset the underperformance that can happen from time to time.

Many typical Americans are also hard-pressed to accurately answer this question: How much money in interest are you being charged for the luxury of using other people's money?

Do you ever check out the front page of your credit card statements? Most people don't. But a recently passed federal statute, the Credit Card Accountability, Responsibility and Disclosure Act signed into law by President Obama in 2010, requires credit card firms to use "plain language in plain sight" on everything relating to your account and to regularly inform you in your statements how long it will take for you to pay off your present balance with interest charges if you only cover the minimum amount due each month. If you haven't taken a good look at the front page of your credit card statements lately, maybe you should. What you see may give you pause about re-evaluating the costs of using other people's money to fulfill your short-term needs or wants.

Do you really grasp what debt is? It's a hole in the ground in which you are standing. You want to build yourself an adequate sized nest egg for your future, and the only way you will start making real progress is to get out of the hole and back onto level ground. Your debt hole isn't even on solid ground. It's more like quicksand that is swallowing up more and more of your income. You're slowly sinking farther into it; you're sinking faster if you have higher interest rates you are paying.

An important first step on the road to achieving your financial goals is knowing the exact depth of the hole you're already in. You also need to know if you are continuing to sink deeper or are you making progress in getting out of the hole. This is critical knowledge. Without it you can't move forward.

Another tenet is spending less than you make every month. We've discussed this before, but it's worth repeating because it is so simple yet so powerful: Spend less than you make every month.

This just means your decisions need to be driven by how much you make and what you need to live on today rather than what you want to make in the future or what you want today that you figure you can pay for later on. A great example is the car. Almost everyone in America has a need for one. There is a dizzying array of vehicles from which you can choose. The range begins around $3,000 for a used but serviceable commuter car all the way up to the most luxurious higher-than-six-figure foreign sedan. The question you need to answer is not which car you want to buy but which car can you afford to purchase. A typical mistake people make early in life that continues well into their working years is basing their car purchasing decisions on what they want rather than what they really need.

When presented with the choice of a $400 a month car payment or a $150 a month car payment, most people will chose the $150 a month car payment for obvious reasons. But when the curtain is lifted on the kind of car you can drive for $150 a month, the average American becomes a little squeamish, even if that vehicle is perfectly adequate and presentable. "I can't be seen driving in that car. What will people think?" In fact, transportation costs for the average U.S. household rose from 15 percent of family income in 1960, to nearly 18 percent in 2009, according to the U.S. Bureau of Labor Statistics Consumer Expenditure Survey. Could it be because Americans' appetite for fancier cars has increased?

Similarly, given the choice of a $1,500 a month payment on a 30-year fixed home mortgage versus a $1,000 a month mortgage payment, the average American will choose the $1,000 a month payment, again for obvious reasons. But once the curtain goes up on what they can afford for $1,000 a month, the average person thinks, "Oh, I want that bigger house with the bigger yard, or that house in the nicer neighborhood or that house that has a built-in pool."

Housing expenditures (mortgage or rent payments) for the average household in America went up from 13 percent of family income in 1960, to 34 percent today.

Interestingly, households belonging to the poor, middle and wealthy classes spend "a huge chunk of their budget [on] housing," according to a National Public Radio "Planet Money" report from August 2012. But figures from the U.S. Bureau of Labor Statistics show the wealthy devote about seven times more of their income to retirement savings than the poor and more than one and a half times above what the middle class contributes.

One reason the poor cannot afford to put as much into retirement is because there are minimum levels of cost to have a roof over your head. They definitely don't have the luxury of choices in how much they can spend on shelter as compared to someone who is very wealthy. However, this makes it even more important for people of limited means to make smart decisions about shelter and transportation. For every extra dollar they spend on housing and transportation, that's one less dollar they can save for their future benefit.

The car and house payment examples are relevant because they usually make up the biggest monthly obligations in the typical person's budget. Equally important is the idea that these payments are usually set in stone; they are fixed, not flexible. After you sign mortgage papers or a purchase contract on a vehicle, what you owe each month is pretty much established for many years. These are examples of financial decisions people make with a lot of forethought as to what they want, but not nearly enough thought about what they need or can afford, and about whether they have other meaningful financial goals they wish to realize that may be limited by the home or car buying decision.

Most people aren't single with no children or other family responsibilities. They can't just think only of themselves. If they're responsible, they must also think of others who depend upon them. So if you have as your goal achieving financial independence for yourself and your loved ones some day, how will you reach that goal if you lock yourself into binding financial contracts for houses and cars that cost too much and that represent huge obstacles to reaching your goal?

Instead of buying a brand new $30,000 vehicle that will commit you to $400 to $500 monthly car payments over the next five or six years, what about choosing a late model, low-mileage used car that is still under warranty but comes with considerably lower monthly payments? In today's real estate market it may be difficult to downsize from a home to which you are already committed. But if there is an opportunity to purchase another house, consider what you can do with an extra $400 or even $700 a month by having a lower mortgage payment. That money could go to pay down other debt, to put towards your future financial independence or a child's college education or to give to the charity of your choice if you are on track with your other financial objectives.

Still another tenet recommended by financial professionals is to focus on acquiring assets that go up and not down in value over time. You can own two kinds of assets. There are those that depreciate or go down in value and those that appreciate or go up in value.

Assets that help you achieve your financial goals by going up in value include traditional investments such as stocks, bonds, mutual funds and real estate. Assets that don't help you achieve your goals because they go down in value start with that brand new car you bought at the auto dealership that made you feel so good. It feels so good, looks so good and smells so good when you prepare to drive it off the lot for the first time to show it off for your friends and neighbors. But the moment it hits the street, that new-smelling car just depreciated by many thousands of dollars. Timeshares are another asset that never go up in value; they will always go down. There are so many developer profits, fees and commissions built into the initial timeshare purchase plus the ongoing annual maintenance costs that make this asset impossible to appreciate. Yes, it's fun to own a timeshare and stay in it. But fun doesn't equate with a good investment decision. Buying a timeshare from the developer when it premieres can cost you $90,000. When you turn around and try to sell it a few years later, it fetches $20,000. As a financial decision, buying a timeshare ranks right up there with buying a new car, unless of course you've already met all your more important financial goals and you can afford it.

The more excited you are to buy an asset, the more you know that it's probably a bad investment. Such moments are when you are typically less rational in making a buying decision than if you go into the decision with a more level headed attitude. Let's go back to the blue jeans purchase at the store. Most people don't start out deciding they're going to pay $200 for a pair of jeans when a $30 pair will serve the same purpose and look just fine. Half of our readers may identify with the $200 jean purchaser. The other half might find paying that much money completely alien. The reality is we're not saying every single clothing purchase you make must be based on the lowest possible price. We know fashion exists and to the extent you can afford more expensive apparel, you should enjoy it. But like all financial matters, if you let your wants and desires outweigh your true needs, you will quickly find yourself with more limited financial resources impeding attainment of your long range financial goals.

Realizing that time is just as powerful an asset as money is another fundamental tenet of becoming financially independent. There is an old Mexican proverb that goes, "There is more time than life." It is used to remind us that you can't choose whether or not you're going to die or even when. It also means that sometimes there are things you want to do in life that you don't have the time to accomplish. That is why it is all the more important to achieve the things you can get done during the time you've been given.

Youth is a great time to be working. You have energy, vigor and resiliency, both mental and physical. It's not a coincidence that nature permits most people to have children during the first third of their lives when they have the energy and strength to keep up with the kids. Most people typically reach their peak earning years in the middle third of their lives. By the time they hit the last third of their lives, if they haven't done what's necessary during the first two-thirds, they face a bigger challenge. So even if you're no longer in your 20s or 30s, all is not lost.

We as authors are mindful about understanding that the average reader of this book is not 20 years old and looking ahead to the luxury of a 40-year or longer career lifespan. It is also important to remember that no matter how young or old you are today, the ability to achieve your financial goals is always going to depend on the ability to postpone instant gratification in order to take financial action towards meeting them.

What does that mean in reality? If you have long had your heart and mind set on a specific retirement age, say 60 years of age, and you find yourself within five to seven years of that deadline woefully unprepared financially, don't give up. One choice you have is applying the asset of the time you still have remaining. If you are in decent health the answer may simply be delaying the date at which you will actually retire to give yourself more time to financially prepare. Another choice has less to do with time and more to do with confronting reality: Still retire at 60, but do so by realizing less monthly income than you had hoped to see.

The lesson here is that time is just as powerful a resource as income. The greatest asset anyone possesses is not money; it's time.

One of the great descriptions of the play of time on financial affairs was attributed to Albert Einstein when he said that compounding interest is "the most powerful force in the universe."

There is a constant debate in the minds of many investors about whether they should put their money in more moderate or conservative long-term financial products or play the market for whatever short-term gains they can realize from more risky propositions. Consistency in sticking with your investments, if they are soundly based and correct in meeting your goals and needs, is always the best course in our view.

Let's say you are offered a choice: You can get handed $1 million in cold hard cash a month from now or receive a penny today and see the amount double each day for a period of 30 days after which you get to keep the resulting lump sum. Well, what would you do? Those who are looking for trick questions might decide on the "penny doubling" option. But many would go for the $1 million at the end of a month; they would be wrong. Here are the simple mathematical calculations:

Day 1: $.01
Day 2: $.02
Day 3: $.04
Day 4: $.08
Day 5: $.16
Day 6: $.32
Day 7: $.64
Day 8: $1.28
Day 9: $2.56
Day 10: $5.12
Day 11: $10.24
Day 12: $20.48
Day 13: $40.96
Day 14: $81.92
Day 15: $163.84
Day 16: $327.68
Day 17: $655.36
Day 18: $1,310.72
Day 19: $2,621.44
Day 20: $5,242.88

Day 21: $10,485.76
Day 22: $20,971.52
Day 23: $41,943.04
Day 24: $83,886.08
Day 25: $167,772.16
Day 26: $335,544.32
Day 27: $671,088.64
Day 28: $1,342,177.28
Day 29: $2,684,354.56
Day 30: $5,368,709.12

The math amounts to petty change at first. But towards the end...well, you can see what is happening. The penny-doubling choice yields you more than five times the $1 million for which you might have otherwise settled. This is how the compounding of interest works for investors. It is only in those later years that the power of compounding becomes so advantageous. Einstein was right.

We obviously can't be guaranteed a magic penny that doubles in value every day. But we do have the power of time working in our favor; it gives us the potential to have the most profound impact on our money.

This exercise simply demonstrates the operation and the benefit of time.

A corollary tenet is setting realistic expectations for yourself. What is realistic for one person may be completely unrealistic for another. We work with thousands of company retirement plan participants through their 401(k) and profit sharing accounts. Most of these employees are newcomers when it comes to financial planning. When we engage in our initial one-on-one conversations, it becomes clear most of them are putting away money into these accounts at a rate that is not set by their own expectations, but rather by the expectations of those around them. They may ask their friend or co-worker, "Hey man, how much are you putting in?" Or they may simply listen to us provide broad, generic guidelines about the percentage of their income they should consider contributing into the retirement account.

As we have repeated time and again, one of the central themes of this book is that everyone's financial goals, needs and conditions are different. But one common denominator for all of us is setting our own concrete expectations of what we can achieve. The average of what most people believe is a realistic contribution to their 401(k) plan is in the range of three to five percent of their gross annual income. The irony is that most people should be contributing much more than that to replace their income at the time of retirement.

Once you create a measurable goal, determine how much you own and owe, the sum total of all your assets and liabilities (debts) Then objectively understand how much time you have on your side: How many more working years are at your disposal. Then focus on acquiring assets that increase in value over time and see how much progress you are making. You may discover that in order to meet your goals it will be necessary to contribute 10 percent of your annual income into saving for the future. However, most people would find jumping all of a sudden from three to 10 percent is completely unrealistic. The cut to their take home income would be so drastic that they literally wouldn't have enough money left over to pay for basic necessities. This could especially be true if the person is just now coming to terms with changing some of his or her former bad financial habits such as overspending.

A better approach to achieving the 10 percent goal, other than engaging in "cold turkey," is doing it gradually over time. Commit yourself to raising the percentage of monthly contributions by one to two percent every six months. That way, you can over time make the adjustment in a more humane and tolerable fashion, yet still achieve the 10 percent goal.

Other examples of people with good intentions but unrealistic expectations are those who find themselves very near the age at which they would love to stop working but discover that their nest egg isn't all they had hoped it would be at that point. Their good intentions are to still fulfill the goal of retiring at a set age. But they go about it by assuming that instead of the more modest rate of return their investments have produced of say 7 percent annually, they are going to shoot for something more like a 12 percent a year return, just to boost the size of their nest egg in a more limited period of time.

It is easy to put pen to paper or finger to calculator to see that a 12 percent rate of return might very well allow someone to retire in five years. Unfortunately, the ability to achieve that rate of return in that limited time frame is almost completely out of the control of the person making the decision. Now he or she is at the mercy of market forces and economic cycles that cannot be influenced by individual investors.

A better solution for this person might be changing two things: Decide to put away a little more money each month in the time you have remaining to work or delay retirement for several years beyond the set goal. Choosing among these options, and weighing how much you do of each, would be exercising more realistic expectations that are within your control.

The next tenet of financial independence follows from the last one: Protecting yourself from risks or eventualities you can't control. You can't control health, disability, economic downturns, loss of employment or other external forces or personal tragedies such as home fires, car accidents or death (of you or your income-contributing spouse), things we don't like to think about.

We can account for these things to the extent that they are all possibilities, but we can be reassured knowing there is a low probability they will occur. Even though the probability is small the possibility does exist. So you should protect yourself to the extent you can from each and every one of these possibilities. How? One way is through adequate levels of the right kind of insurance. Life insurance, for instance, is one of the most attainable and affordable ways to transfer the risk away from your back and onto the back of a large, financially stable insurance company. Still, the experience with real people in our profession tells us there is an alarming number of people who have inadequate insurance, whether it be life insurance or other types. Many people have none even though they have dependents and assets that would be at risk

Many people are less concerned about becoming disabled than dying at an earlier age. Yet statistically you have a much higher chance of becoming disabled for a period of six months than suffering a premature death. Check out this data on the chances of disability compiled by the Council for Disability Awareness, a nonprofit group dedicated to educating Americans about the widespread and increasing incidence of disability and how it can financially impact individuals and families.

– A little more than one quarter of the people who are 20 years old today will become disabled at some point in their lives before retirement.

– More than 36 million Americans, approximately 12 percent of the public, have been classified as disabled, with more than 50 percent of them stricken during their career life spans between the ages of 18 and 64.

– More than 5 percent of U.S. workers, some 8.3 million disabled workers, were the recipients of Social Security Disability Insurance (SSDI) benefits in March 2011.

– Disabled workers in their 20s, 30s and 40s receiving SSDI benefits in December 2010 numbered more than 2.5 million.

Here are some additional insights into reality from the Council for Disability Awareness.

– A typical 35-year old woman who is 5'4" tall, weighs 125 pounds, doesn't smoke, has a healthy lifestyle and works primarily in an office with some physical duties outdoors has a 24 percent chance of contracting a disability that will linger for three months or longer during the course of her working years. There is a 38 percent chance her disability will go on for five years or longer. Eighty-two months is the average period of time a disability will last for someone like this woman. (By the way, if the woman is a smoker and weighs 160 pounds, she has a 41 percent risk of a disability lasting three months or longer.)

– A typical 35-year old man who is 5'10" tall, weighs 170 pounds, doesn't smoke, boasts a healthy lifestyle and mostly works at an office job with some physical responsibilities outside has a 21 percent chance of being disabled for three months or longer during his career life span. There is also a 38 percent chance he will be disabled for five years or longer. He also faces an average period of disability that will last 82 months. (If this man smokes and weighs 210 pounds, he has a 45 percent chance of being disabled for three months or longer.)

The message? Get disability insurance.

There is another form of risk against which you can exert some control. When it comes to your investment nest egg, our industry is known for the ever-present mantra we repeat that investment returns are not guaranteed; you can lose all or a portion of your investment to market forces. Adequately diversifying your investment portfolio can both keep your nest egg intact and enable you to keep your sanity when the markets get dicey, which happens all too frequently. Although diversifying your investments can't prevent your portfolio from going down in value, it can help keep your nest egg from suffering large, potentially life-altering downturns.

We find people who adopt their own version of diversification as opposed to proper diversification. For example, just because someone owns five different mutual funds does not ensure he or she is diversified. Many of those mutual funds could own a lot of the same or similar stocks. The most recent well-known and obvious example of many people falsely believing they had diversity in their portfolios occured in the late 1990s with the Internet and technology stock market bubble. These stocks went up in value at such a rapid pace that people almost became addicted to them and the big profits they "promised." They fooled themselves into believing that if they owned stock in 10 different high-tech companies, perhaps by way of holding five aggressive growth mutual funds, they had adequately dispersed their investment risk. Then reality became painfully apparent as the economy slowed and the tech bubble burst. Almost all of those high-tech assets dramatically fell in unison, destroying tens of billions of dollars in people's collective nest eggs.

One way to truly diversify is understanding that your investment portfolios should be comprised of a wide selection of appreciating and/or income generating assets, each one performing independently of the other. There are an infinite number of risks against which you can't easily protect yourself. This is important to remember because there is only one risk against which you can *easily* protect yourself: Running out of money before you run out of life.

The last tenet along the path of becoming financially independent entails taking a little time out each month to learn something new and important about personal financial planning. Numerous studies have shown a direct correlation between literacy in personal financial planning and enjoying financial success in life by building a larger nest egg, having less debt and achieving financial independence more quickly.

"The financially savvy are more likely to plan and to succeed in their planning, and they rely on formal methods such as retirement calculators, retirement seminars and financial experts instead of family/relatives or co-workers," according to a 2011 study, "Financial Literacy and Planning: Implications for Retirement Wellbeing," by Annamaria Lusardi with the George Washington

School of Business and Olivia S. Mitchell from the University of Pennsylvania's Wharton School of Business. After sampling a nationally representative group of older Americans, Lusardi and Mitchell reported that "only two-thirds of the respondents understand compound interest," despite the long-ago observance by Einstein. "This is a discouraging finding inasmuch as this generation in its 50s and 60s has made many important financial decisions over its lifetime." Additionally, "only half of the [older] respondents know that holding a single company stock implies a riskier return than a stock mutual fund" where risk is spread out among an array of different kinds of companies. One third of respondents answered that they didn't know the answer to this stock risk question while 13 percent picked the wrong answer.

The authors concluded that "financial illiteracy is systemic" among this age group. "Such individuals often fail to understand key financial concepts, particularly relating to bonds, stocks, mutual funds and the working of compound interest." What's more, "these people often do not understand loans (and in particular, mortgages)." Other studies of high school students and adults who are working "revealed a widespread lack of knowledge of fundamental economic concepts," according to the authors.

The sad state of financial illiteracy in this country is why "Bernie Madoff and other scammers have been successful [and why] millions of Americans went in over their heads with mortgages they didn't understand," according to Elliot Raphaelson, a one-time bank executive, university professor and court mediator aiding people out of financial disputes who was quoted in a 2012 article published by Tribune Media Services.

One of the most stressful aspects of living is trying to contend with your own finances. How many marriages do we know about that have ended, or almost ended, over financial differences and the inability to communicate and be on the same page when it comes to agreeing about money? Ignorance is not bliss when it involves your finances. Being financially ignorant is the best way to ensure you will never be financially stress free. Focusing on your physical health is important. But the benefits of focusing on your financial literacy in order to improve your mental well being, that is incalculable.

This is why one of the main features of FlexScore is its comprehensive On-line Learning Center. It can be accessed at www.FlexScore.com. The FlexScore On-line Learning Center is available anywhere in the world at no cost. This may not seem such an earth-shattering opportunity since you can find much good information about personal financial planning for free all over the Internet. Yet the relevancy and down-to-earth approach with which we present our information makes becoming financially literate simple.

CHAPTER SIX

Why Your Current 'Advisor' Has Never Done This For You

"No enemy is worse than bad advice."

— **Sophocles**, ancient Greek playwright

If the financial planning services available through FlexScore are so great, why don't most financial advisors already provide them? Until now, an industry standard for supplying comprehensive financial planning advice didn't exist. There was no unified method for most advisors in our field to help you with all things financial.

Lack of a uniform industry standard once made it difficult for banks and other creditors to know how reliably applicants would make repayments if they were issued home mortgages or other loans. Lenders didn't have a way to objectively determine people's credit worthiness: Whether or not they should lend money, and whether or not borrowers pay their bills on time.

Then, beginning in the1960s, the Fair Isaac Corporation invented the FICO© credit risk score (now known as myFICO©) that came into widespread use in the financial services industry. myFICO© lets the credit and lending markets quickly and objectively understand a person's credit worthiness. It has dramatically expanded access to credit by consumers. (Whether that is a good or bad thing for the country is still up in the air.) In any case, myFICO© quickly became recognized as the industry standard for lenders to understand their clients and make their decisions.

FlexScore is going to become the equivalent of the myFICO© score when it comes to how the financial services business will help more Americans. Like myFICO©, FlexScore helps people know where they stand with their personal finances as they travel along the path of meeting their goals.

The personal finance industry today is an amalgam of industries that were once viewed as independent of each other. In years past, banks were just banks. The insurance industry only wrote insurance policies. Investment advisors only handled stocks, bonds and mutual funds. Mortgage companies and traditional banks were the only entities that could give you a mortgage. Much of this compartmentalization sprang from the Banking Act of 1933, called the Glass-Steagall Act after its congressional authors. It said if you're going to offer financial services, you must remain within that discipline where your expertise resides. For instance, bankers could only do banking and insurers could only do insurance. The Gramm-Leach-Bliley Act of 1999 repealed the Glass-Steagall Act, although many people argued the 1933 prohibitions on straying outside your narrow field of financial endeavor had already been substantially eroded by lax interpretations on the part of U.S. banking regulators. These constraints were abandoned because most financial services companies were not only pressing to get their hands on related sides of the financial industry; they were already conducting business that way.

The most famous example was CitiBank. It was the result of a marriage between Travelers, the giant insurance company, and CitiBank, the giant banking institution. Added to the mix was a prestigious investment firm called Solomon Smith Barney. Together, they fashioned the largest financial services company the world had ever seen. (We got our professional start by advising people on their personal finances at Solomon Smith Barney and Morgan Stanley Dean Witter.) Formation of Solomon Smith Barney precipitated the repeal of the Glass-Steagall Act in 1999.

Repeal of these walls separating various aspects of financial services was potentially good in theory, but it hasn't worked out so well for the consumer in practice. The consumer hasn't benefited as much as the industry has. Financial advisors ended up offering services they didn't know much about; too often they didn't have expertise in the subject matter about which they were counseling their clients. If I'm a specialist in market investments talking to my clients about sophisticated insurance policies that I don't fully understand, how am I properly serving them? I am motivated to sell my clients those products that yield the most lucrative profits for my company or myself; that will best serve my interests, but not necessarily the best interests of my clients.

This reality is why industry standards have never been set up to mitigate these inequities. FlexScore performs that function. It shows consumers how to protect themselves in a way the industry presently does not by recommending action steps involving a variety of financial service disciplines based on what people objectively determine is in their own best interests given their unique circumstances. It takes into account all of your financial "moving parts" and doesn't just allow for decisions to be made simply by evaluating a narrow slice of your financial pie.

Let's walk through three separate scenarios created by three different portions of the financial services industry. They all involve a 45-year old middle-income client, married with two minor children who just inherited $100,000. She has sizable consumer debt and recognizes she has not yet started saving for retirement, which is her primary goal in deciding what to do with her newfound money.

Scenario 1. She first walks into the office of an insurance agent recommended by a friend. The insurance agent does his job as an insurance agent. He asks the client about the insurance policies she presently holds. The client has some life insurance; the agent recommends she get some more. There is no disability insurance because the client has always balked at the cost. But since she arrives at the office with a pot of $100,000, disability insurance is now within reach. Since investing for the future is the main reason the client is seeking out the insurance agent, the agent suggests a variable or universal life insurance policy, one part insurance and the other part investment, that will ideally help to grow the client's money and solve the problem of her being both underinsured and behind in her retirement planning.

These recommendations in and of themselves may be appropriate for this particular client. But since the client's overall goals or other financial needs are not being probed, the insurance agent may be putting the cart before the horse. The agent is primarily compensated through the commissions he realizes from the insurance policies he sells. A significant portion of the premiums paid on policies is used to compensate the agents. Therefore, agents have an incentive to place the biggest and costliest insurance policies their clients can afford.

Nothing is said about whether the client has created a will, trust or estate plan. Nothing is asked or said about the consumer debt she carries. And as for her tax situation, forget about it.

Scenario 2. Now this same 45-year old woman walks into her local bank and tries to deposit the $100,000. The teller asks, "Would you like to talk with one of our financial advisors to learn about what you can do with all this money?" The bank financial advisor does the job of a bank financial advisor, which is to quickly inquire about the customer's financial needs and goals. Most of the time in this kind of situation a thorough financial needs and goals assessment is not offered or performed.

The person to whom customers are referred at the bank is often an entry-level financial advisor without the training and experience of a more seasoned professional. This bank employee acts more in the capacity of a sales person than a consultant. What the employee sells customers is limited by what's on the shelf the employee has to offer. Expensive investment products such as variable annuities and high-commission mutual funds are frequently what are on their shelf. A variable annuity is an investment product sponsored by investment and insurance companies that traditionally has high internal expenses buried within the product; that means you as a customer don't know how much you're paying unless you read a 150-page legal document called a prospectus. The companies that compile these prospectuses know 99 out of 100 people won't read them. High commission mutual funds are investments where the person who sells it to you gets a hefty commission.

Bank financial advisor employees typically earn very small salaries, just enough to get by. They usually make commissions, in smaller amounts than the insurance sales people earn, on each bank product in which they convince customers to invest.

Keep in mind that no one at the bank asks this woman with $100,000 about her insurance needs because the bank doesn't sell that product. The client also isn't asked whether she has a will, trust or estate plan in place. And there are no questions raised about her consumer debt.

Scenario 3. Our lady finally strides into the local branch of a major Wall Street investment firm with her $100,000 after being referred by her wealthy uncle who uses the same company. There, the financial advisor inquires a lot about the potential client's risk tolerance, her capacity to assume investment risk, as well as her past experience investing. The brokerage house advisor wants to know where the woman's other money is located. He seems disappointed to learn that the only money the client has available to invest with the company is the $100,000 inheritance, and the only other large items on her balance sheet are a home mortgage and consumer debt. Some leading Wall Street investment firms have compensation policies in place that say if new accounts amount to less than $250,000, any fees or commissions generated by those accounts will not be shared with the local advisor. Why? These Wall Street companies prefer to deal with more well-to-do people, those with more than $250,000 to invest.

The best thing this advisor has to offer our lady is the firm's proprietary product. In other words, the client will have to invest her money in the company's own in-house investment product that consists of mutual funds where the investment firm shares revenues with the mutual fund company that invests the money. Our client can ask to invest in other custom products the investment company offers, but the odds are that the client won't know what to ask for. Even if she does, the advisor probably won't want to take her on as a client or spend much time with her because the advisor will not personally benefit from any fees or commissions from this account.

The Wall Street firm advisor has an advantage over the insurance agent and bank employee: He may be able to offer many of the same products the other two can, albeit without as much expertise on insurance and banking products. The Wall Street advisor primarily makes money based on the business model known as "assets under management." This is where clients get charged an annual percentage of the account value to manage the account. It runs the gamut from 1 to 3 percent.

Let's say our client invests her $100,000 inheritance in a mutual fund offered by the investment company. The financial advisor's charge for managing the money might be 2 percent annually. The fee is typically assessed quarterly. As the $100,000 grows or declines in value over time depending on how the investment fares, the quarterly fee percentage remains the same. You can quickly see that the business model for most Wall Street companies is to acquire and manage the most assets possible. So they can't be meeting all day with $100,000 clients. In order to remain profitable with the limited amount of time all of us have in the day, their best bet is to focus on attracting the largest and wealthiest clients they can.

Once again, no advice is solicited or offered at the Wall Street investment house about a will, trust or estate plan or whether the client should do something about her consumer debt.

In reality, none of the financial recommendations from these three scenarios are necessarily bad. The fact is that none of them were necessarily made in the best interest of the client. The insurance agent will sell her insurance. The bank employee will sell her a product that comes with a high commission. The Wall Street company advisor will sell her his firm's proprietary product. Each one of them believes their solutions are best for the client's situation and will provide the best help they can. Actually, the best solution would result from a true holistic approach, taking fully into account our client's individual financial circumstance plus her needs and goals. None of the financial advisors at these three shops took the time to adequately and comprehensively make that determination.

None of these three compensation models is inherently wrong for the client. However, the compensation models of the people doing the selling lead most clients to certain products and solutions, depending on the office into which they walk. Too often, the products offered and the accompanying compensation models create conflicts of interest. They may or may not be in the best interest of clients given their unique situations. The financial services industry's intentions are good. But the way it is set up and exists today, the industry doesn't have the capacity to provide objective assessments and recommendations individually tailored to each client's needs and goals, especially if the client does not come in the door with a sizable portfolio in hand.

Now the financial services industry can offer that capacity with FlexScore.

Many people have the ability to place the words "financial advisor" on their business cards. But the term in and of itself doesn't mean the financial advisor will act independently and with the clients' best interest in mind.

From day one, our firm in the Central Valley of California followed the principle that we are beholden to only one entity, our clients. We represent our clients to the financial world rather than represent specific subsets of the financial world to our clients, meaning banks, insurance companies or Wall Street firms.

We left a big Wall Street financial firm to found our own independent advice practice because we saw the advantage our clients enjoyed with us working for them rather than us working for a financial institution. We're not compensated by up-front commissions or proprietary products that skew our ability to make objective recommendations. This isn't to say that all financial advisors make decisions solely based on their methods of compensation. But there needs to be an objective way to balance an individual's true needs with the financial services industry's ability to meet them. FlexScore solves this problem.

We also became convinced that our business model must be replicated throughout our industry. This model must be made available to all Americans, no matter the size of their debts, the worth of their assets, the complexity of their finances or the way they define financial success.

FlexScore gives you the ability to work much more effectively with your financial advisor. Or you can choose to use FlexScore without the aid of advisors. Either way, FlexScore helps you by taking complex financial planning principles and breaking them down to small bites everyone can understand and identify with. FlexScore is an on-line platform that provides the same services we supply the clients, big or small, we serve each day through our practice.

Industry regulations have offered half measures and bandage

solutions devised to remove some conflicts of interest confronting consumers across the years. One such solution is the ability to trade stocks at increasingly lower costs. Some financial plans offered by banks and Wall Street firms refer people to departments within their companies that handle planning when their advisors don't have the competence to do it themselves. The planning can be offered for free in anticipation that it will produce more opportunities to sell clients high-cost sophisticated financial products sponsored by the same firm.

There are too many conflicts of interest that never go away. What's important is that the consumer understands whether the advice is genuinely offered in his or her best interest or whether it is being provided for the purpose of compensating the people selling the product and the company employing the salespersons. If the answer is the former, then why doesn't the advisor use a system like FlexScore? It is because until now this industry-standard tool didn't exist for them. It does now.

Financial planning software other than FlexScore does exist and is available to any financial advisor who chooses to use it. The software allows advisors to succinctly list clients' assets and debts, categorize their investments and touch on issues such as insurance and estate planning. But at the end of the day, this software ends up becoming fancy comprehensive spreadsheets without offering any solutions that translate into easy to understand courses of action. Existing financial planning software leaves those functions up to financial advisors. This deficiency explains why conflicts of interest caused by compensation methods and proprietary products still persist.

FlexScore is different because it ranks the importance of the financial actions you should be taking based on your particular needs, wants and desires as you prioritize them yourself. What if you had your own F-16 fighter jet to take you to and from work? It's a convenient and swift way to travel, if only you know how to fly such a sophisticated aircraft. FlexScore lets you navigate through the intricacies of analysis and multiple products and solutions that exist in today's complex financial planning world, only it is all being piloted by you.

Conversations with financial advisors frequently revolve around what they believe you came in to talk with them about. The subject depends on the type of financial office you enter: Insurance agency, bank or investment firm. The advisors' goal, maybe, is to steer the subject matter to that which they have an interest in selling you. The Wall Street advisor presents you with fancy charts and talks about the Dow Jones Industrial Average and other stock market-related background noise. But you don't have much control over what happens in that arena. The investment firm doesn't either. Neither one of you can influence or even predict with any certainty what's going to happen. The frustration sets in when, in meeting after meeting or call after call, you hear the same mantra: "Stay the course; in the long term everything will be fine. History shows it always gets better." While those are good ideas to remember, none of them solve the immediate problem of what can you do today to get closer to realizing your financial goals tomorrow.

FlexScore takes the background noise out of the equation and places directly in front of you those things you can do now to actually improve your circumstance, no matter what your goals happen to be.

This is a huge advantage for both consumers of financial planning services and for the financial planning industry itself. FlexScore changes the focus and conversation from what's going on in the stock and bond markets and the economy to what are the steps you need to take to make financial progress based on action items that will improve your FlexScore. It concentrates your attention on the things that matter the most: A holistic and complete view of your financial situation and not just what's presently happening with your investment assets. It lets your advisor work to genuinely improve your financial condition over time. Instead of talking about how particular investment strategies have performed during the last quarter, your advisor can focus on showing you where your FlexScore, and therefore your path to financial independence, has gone in the same period of time.

The result will be better-informed clients who are confident in the counsel being provided by their advisors and the knowledge that both clients and advisors are working together to solve the clients' financial puzzles. Clients will feel better. Advisors will be doing more. Because clients feel less frustrated and more confident they are doing the right thing financially, many more referrals will come the advisors' way. In our experience employing the FlexScore process every day, clients no longer worry about things they can't control when their needs are being met and well served, when they are more knowledgeable and when they have a better understanding of their financial situation and direction.

In a way, FlexScore is analogous to the medical specialist to whom you are referred by your general practitioner. The specialist diagnoses your malady and prescribes a medical course of treatment. You work with your general practitioner who performs the requisite follow-up tests and ensures you're following the treatment regimen the specialist prescribed. The specialist can enhance the relationship between the patient and the general practitioner just as FlexScore enhances the relationship between the client and his or her independent financial advisor, if there is one. FlexScore can also be fully implemented on your own.

Let's get real. It isn't fun when financial advisors and their clients constantly discuss assets, liabilities and, God forbid, establishing and keeping to a budget. All of those things involve hard work.

Zumba is the latest international fitness craze, combining Latin and other forms of music with an enjoyable yet productive system of working out and getting into better physical shape. Before you arrive at your Zumba class, you know you can do better with your exercising. Both your spouse and your doctor have reminded you of that fact. But looking at yourself in the mirror every day and knowing it is a big, uphill battle makes excuses not to exercise easy to come by. Postponing until tomorrow the inevitable physical activity that makes you sweat and hurt a little bit is easy to do, even if tomorrow frequently doesn't come.

Zumba helps because it is fun, because music is involved and because you're doing it in conjunction with other people. Zumba makes it easier for you to do what you know you should be doing. It helps you increase your frequency of physical activity and your level of physical fitness.

Just like you don't have to be a professional salsa dancer to benefit from Zumba, you don't need to be a millionaire or a financial planning authority to benefit from FlexScore. Like Zumba, FlexScore helps you do what you know you should be doing by making it fun. Our industry is not known for fun. It's known for staid, button-down approaches to finances and life. That's not FlexScore. FlexScore is real and responsible financial planning. It just happens to be fun too.

Even before picking up this book, you knew you should be more responsible about using your money. You knew you should be better protecting your loved ones. You knew you should be doing a better job of planning for the future and taking action towards achieving your overarching financial goals. Yet without the help of the action steps to make short-term progress one step at a time, as represented by the points you earn and feel rewarded for achieving through FlexScore, delaying the instant gratification that is key to achieving financial success isn't all that fun. It's more fun to focus only on your immediate wants and desires. It's a lot less fun to sit down with a financial advisor and seriously think about the security of your future.

FlexScore helps you do what you already know you should be doing, and it lets you enjoy the process while you do it.

CHAPTER SEVEN

What's Your Direction: What Matters and What Doesn't?

"If you do not change direction, you may end up where you are heading."

—Lau Tzu, Chinese Taoist philosopher

In previous chapters we spoke about one of the core tenets of becoming financially independent: Having realistic expectations. Too many people believe because there is a possibility of something happening, simply hoping it will happen increases the odds it will occur. Frankly, possibility and probability are two completely different things. Harboring an expectation that defies reality only sets you up for failure because you completely overlook all the hurdles that will come your way. Nowhere does this reality strike home more than when your unrealistic expectation falls along the road to financial independence.

Setting goals is a central principle of planning. If those goals aren't achievable, no amount of wishful thinking short of divine intervention will help you achieve them. People's religious beliefs aside, we have to do what we can under our own understanding and not rely on the divine to ensure we're heading in the right financial direction. So this chapter continues covering those things that matter in moving you towards financial independence and exposing those myths of actions and behaviors that so many people think are relevant when they are not.

One popular myth is that we must obtain a very high rate of return on our investments over a lifetime in order to become financially secure. For purposes of this discussion, let's define a high rate of return as somewhere north of 10 percent. Earning a 10 percent rate of return is doing very well. It's achievable, but to realize an average return in that neighborhood over the period of a lifetime would require a willingness to accept a pretty high tolerance for risk that many people are not prepared to accept when it comes to their own money.

We all know people who are risk-takers, whether the risk involves driving too fast, participating in extreme sports or partying a little too hard on the weekend. We all know the personality type that demonstrates more tolerance for risk in everyday life. But that tolerance doesn't always apply when it comes to placing at risk your own prospects for financial success. When it comes time to invest their money, most people immediately focus on what they see as the daily fluctuations of the stock market. There is the real risk of losing all or a major portion of their investments; an investment made unwisely can suddenly shrink to less than the investor thought it was worth, or the value can drop to zero.

The Great Recession that Americans began witnessing in 2008 was accompanied by a disastrous stock market reaction between the peak of the market in October 2007, and the trough or low point in March 2009. As measured by the Standard & Poor's 500 index , the benchmark of the top 500 public companies in America, that part of the market lost 57 percent of its value during this economic downturn.

Imagine if in the summer of 2007, you set up a very well-thought-out financial plan. You were going to invest your portfolio and consistently save on a monthly basis towards reaching a goal more than 15 or 20 years away, all with the expectation of a 10 percent return. The 10 percent return required you to place a large portion of your money in the stock market, where higher potential risks are normal. Within about 18 months after making your initial investment, you could have suffered a 57 percent loss. This would have set you back considerably. Even with investments based on a more modest seven percent return, you would not have completely escaped the stock market reversal.

These setbacks occur from time to time in the stock market. We can blame the housing market collapse. We can blame government regulation or lack of regulation. We can blame corporate irresponsibility or Wall Street. At the end of the day, losses will happen because of any number of variables or a combination of them. That's the problem with trying to achieve a higher rate of return as the only strategy in becoming financially independent. So much has to go right and so little has to go wrong that you end up relying on luck or happenstance as much as anything.

The alternative of a high-risk-buy-and-hope approach is a more measured buy-and-hold approach. With the latter, you try to achieve a rate of return that is more within your tolerance for risk. If you frequently feel worry, regret or remorse after making a financial decision, then this approach might work best for you. Those are symptoms of an investor with a lower tolerance for financial risk. Before setting your goals and putting your money in higher-risk investment strategies, take an honest measurement of your own personality, your past investment behavior and your personal risk tolerance. If achieving your goal requires that you build up $1 million at the end of the next 20 years and it depends on achieving a 10 percent return on investment, then you must fully understand what that means; the risks you are assuming could be substantial. A simple financial calculator on some website may say if you earn a 10 percent investment return you'll make your goal. But you need to know you can stomach the investment risk. Instead, find a rate of return that correlates with the risk you're willing to assume over time without losing sleep or constantly fretting. If a more cautious investment strategy means you will end up short of your financial goal, find a way to increase the amount of income you are willing to put towards reaching that goal rather than attempting to abide by the emotional uncertainty associated with striving for a higher rate of return.

Is it really worth spending 20 years of sleepless nights reaching a goal that may be too ambitious for your investment personality, not to mention jeopardizing part or all of your investment in the process?

There are so many real life examples of people who we've seen make investment decisions that are completely wrong for them, often against our best advice.

A prime example of the overconfident investor is another of our clients, a business owner in his 50s, married with adult children. He possessed great business acumen and had done well with his company because he thoroughly understood his industry and controlled his professional domain. His mistake was convincing himself that his successful business sense would directly translate into what would work in the investment world. He grossly overestimated his ability to analyze investments and endure the accompanying risk. He knew relatively little about the complex history of the stock market, which is where he wanted to invest.

This gentleman approached us, asking us to invest his $1 million Individual Retirement Account, or IRA. "I want you guys to come up with half the ideas [on what he should invest in] and I'll come up with the other half," he said. So he wanted us to manage $500,000 of his portfolio and he would manage the rest. His directive almost set up a contest of sorts to see if he could do better than we could in managing his investments.

We aren't so conceited as to think that we have a monopoly on all the good ideas. This man was certainly capable of coming up with his own investment strategy and successfully managing it, to the extent of even earning a higher rate of return than we could produce. We tried to clearly explain he should not view our endeavor as a contest because the effort has no ending time frame. Most contests or games have a set beginning and an end. Our client looked at it as a way to perhaps have some fun, but with serious money. We didn't feel this was the right way for him to go about reaching financial independence.

"You're right, you're right," he replied. "Let's just say you do as well as you can and I'll do the best I can. I'm okay with investment risk. So please feel free to give me your best ideas."

He set his goal for his half of the $1 million as achieving a 15 percent rate of return. He asked us to do the same. We knew from long experience that this sort of high rate of return encompassed a tremendous degree of risk with interim ups and downs that the average investor simply can't stand. We counseled the client to make sure he understood what he was taking on. He avowed that he fully understood it. We said over a longer period of time we might be able to generate a rate of return averaging 11 or 12 percent, but that 15 percent was probably too lofty of a goal.

In 2004, we set out to invest our half of his $1 million. We fashioned a portfolio of diversified aggressive investment strategies. They mostly involved stock market-oriented high-growth and international companies that inherently retained a great deal of volatility in their day-to-day prices. Fluctuations in value of between 10 and 15 percent over short periods of time, a month or two, were not uncommon. If, for instance, you bought one of these stocks at $10 a share, within 30 days you could see it drop to $8.50 a share. Sometimes the share price would not come back up for months at a time. On the flip side, it could go up from $10 to $11.50 a share in the same period. Short-term volatility is very normal for these sorts of investments. Yet in our opinion these were the most suitable assets to own to gain the rate of return our guy was seeking.

Our strategy mostly utilized mutual funds, which spread his investment risk out over stocks from hundreds of different companies that make up the funds. This somewhat mitigated the risk of serious loss because we weren't putting all of our eggs in one or only a few baskets. If a few of the hundreds of companies in the mutual funds tanked, it wouldn't sink his entire investment.

The portfolio we put together began to achieve rates of return we thought were pretty good: nine or 10 percent after the first year, six or seven percent in the second year and 11 or 12 percent in the third year.

Meanwhile, our client invested his $500,000 with individual stocks of very specific companies he thought he knew everything about. Most of them were either technology or biotechnology firms or health care-related companies that, in his view, were the wave of the future. The research on which he relied consisted of charts of these stocks' most recent performance over the last one-year period. The high-tech stock market bubble had already burst in the year 2000, so he assumed the research he was using was enough for him to foresee the future. His analysis process went something like this: Well, this company's stock price has gone up by 50 percent in the last 12 months. Therefore, it will go up another 50 percent in the next 12 months.

So he bought stock in firms that had essentially performed far above average in the most recent past. He was doing something we always caution our clients against: Buying high rather than buying low. The old investment adage of buying low and selling high means at its core that you should look for investments with future potential and buy them at a price before that potential is realized. In other words, buy the stock at a bargain price before it goes up.

Our guy was doing the opposite. Somehow he felt there was an inevitable momentum in a stock price having gone up so much and so quickly. He thought he was ingenious in picking these stocks because their prices would continue to rise. Yet he was clearly not buying bargains. He was beginning to buy overpriced and overrated investments that had little room for more upward movement. Inevitably, almost every single stock he purchased quickly began to move down after it found a home in his investment portfolio.

The client realized that in order to make a 15 percent return he would have to take risks, and he was willing to do that, which is fine. He just didn't do it in a very smart way. There are smart ways to take risks and there are not-so-smart ways to take risks. Our client's overconfidence in his business judgment convinced him to take not so smart risks in order to achieve an unrealistic rate of return.

He lost $100,000 of the $500,000 portfolio he was handling during the first year of his investing. That meant in order to reach his goal of an overall 15 percent rate of return (his goal and not ours), our client needed to achieve more than a 15 percent return rate in future years just to overcome his initial losses. It comes down to simple mathematics. It matters whether you are trying to achieve a realistic rate of return versus a lofty rate because math counts. Here's how it works.

Let's say you have $100,000 to invest and do very poorly with your investment choices in the first year. You lose half of your money, thus suffering a 50 percent loss in value. The average person, not thinking through the math of the situation, believes if you lose 50 percent one year, all you need to do to make up for the loss is simply earn 50 percent on your investment in the next year and you'll be back to even.

Now look at it in real dollars. After one year of unsuccessful investing, your $100,000 is now worth only $50,000. If all you achieve in the subsequent year of investing is a 50 percent rate of return, which would be a fantastic achievement, you're only going to get back up to $75,000, not $100,000. In order to turn your $50,000 back into $100,000, you need to make a 100 percent rate of return over a fairly short period of time. That only takes you back to where you began before the initial loss. It also begs the question: Is a 100 percent rate of return realistic in a short amount of time if we've already conceded that a 15 percent return rate over the same short period is not realistic?

The point we're making is achieving a consistent rate of return with the least amount of volatility or risk is far more important than trying for some sort of double digit return rate that a web site's financial calculator tells you will meet your goals. Yes, the math employed by the calculator is correct. But what may not be correct is your ability to achieve a rate of return that is too high for your own peace of mind or that is just plain unattainable.

Let's get back to our client the business owner. We counseled him that individual company stocks are extremely risky unless you know exactly what you're buying and why you're buying them. The fact that a company's stock has recently gone up a lot in value (his criteria in picking stocks) is not a reason to buy it. It may be a reason to closely examine the company as a first step.

Not having done so well the first time around, this business owner thought he would use the same tools we employed. So he started putting his money into mutual funds.

That led to his next mistake. In buying mutual funds, he used the same kind of investment thinking that brought him to buy stocks in individual high-tech firms: He bought mutual funds that were invested in high-tech companies. He did mitigate the risk of losing large portions of his money should one company's stock fail. Unfortunately, once again he picked high-tech mutual funds because they boasted the highest rate of return in the recent past, namely the last 12 months.

It's one thing if a mutual fund has a long, tenured record of performance, say over the past 10 years. But if it is showing well only in the last 12 months, it might be more because of luck rather than sound choices made over time by management. What our client effectively did was remove the chance of losing a good deal of his money should one stock fail, but he still ended up with a very shabby investment strategy by limiting his choices to last year's winners. The law of averages prevails in situations such as this: If an investment strategy has done very well in the recent past, the following years might bring the average down to even or even below average performance. A wine grape vineyard in one appellation may produce very good quality grapes one year; they may not be so good the following year. It can have to do with factors that *can't* be controlled, such as weather, and factors that *can* be controlled, such as attention and management. We do know over a long period of time that good years will average out against bad years and overall hopefully there will be more good years than bad years, overall.

The secret in the investment realm isn't making a high rate of return. It's simply making a rate of return that keeps your money moving in the right direction as consistently as possible.

Our client actually did reasonably well given how he selected the investments he controlled: High tech mutual funds based on their last 12 months of performance. By well we mean he didn't make money since he ended up about even. But he didn't lose money either, which, considering his amateur thinking, was a mark of success.

Just over three years after we began investing half of the client's original funds our $500,000 turned into a little more than $600,000. His half of his money dropped from $500,000 to $400,000, and stayed there. So at the end of three years, his initial $1 million ended up being about $1 million, when accounting for his losses and our gains. His net effect was he didn't lose any money, but he still had a long way to go in achieving his financial goals.

Oh, in the meantime his experience struggling to achieve a 15 percent rate of return saddled him with years of stress, worry and battle wounds putting up with the vagaries of the investment market. By the time he was back to even, we were on the edge of experiencing the dramatic losses of value in the stock market downturn that was around the corner in 2008. At the end of that year, our client decided that attempting to "get rich quick" wasn't worth the risk or the grief and decided to turn over his entire portfolio to us.

A different example of what to avoid while investing your money was presented by an office manager. She was in her mid-50s when she came to us and hailed from a very different financial situation. Others managed the $250,000 she had already saved through a retirement account provided by her employer. Her company made the investment decisions so she didn't have to worry about them. Our client represented herself as someone with an interest in investing and making her own decisions. But she didn't have very much experience in the stock market. At this time (it was the year 2000) in the wake of a very hot stock market, she wanted to dip her toe into the world of investing. So, like our businessman client, this lady wanted to carve out a portion of her portfolio with which to make her own investment decisions while we invested the rest, what she called "the serious money."

She decided to slice off $50,000 of her $250,000, what she termed her "fun account." The good news was this client did have realistic expectations of what she thought she could make. She was shooting for an eight percent investment return. We told her that was achievable in that she could give us directions for investing her $50,000, while we invested the other $200,000 using the strategies we believed were best.

Her directions were to put the $50,000 into this or that mutual fund; she also had a few stock investments to try. Fortunately, she chose quite a few so-called "blue chip" stocks that nearly everyone would be comfortable holding. What we soon discovered was that our client had an uncanny ability to do exactly the wrong thing at the wrong time.

There were times, over a few weeks or a month, when everything in the stock market was performing lousy. During these periods she would call our office and instruct us to sell all the investments from the $50,000 of her portfolio that she was controlling. She was acting, as our client put it, "to protect my money and get out of the stock market and wait until things get better."

We always asked her, "How do you define when things get better?" After all, we added, "No bell will ring to inform you that things are now better and you can get back in the stock market." We added that even with all the data and access to information we possess as professional investment advisors, there is no 100 percent accurate indicator that lets people know when to get in and out of the market in order to protect their capital.

"I feel it in my bones that it's time to get out," this lady would reply, "and therefore I'll know when it's time to get back in."

For a period of a few months her $50,000 portion sat in cash in some money market account making a small amount of interest. Meantime, the stock market and all of her former blue chip stocks improved and their prices went up, even though she didn't own them anymore. By then she felt it "in her bones" and called to instruct us to get back in the market.

Another few months went by and stock market volatility being what it is, the same scenario repeated itself. The market experienced a slight downturn. Even though we deemed the investments owned by our client to be good quality stocks, their prices temporarily deteriorated. What happened to our client? She got another bad feeling in her bones, called us and said, "I shouldn't have gotten back in. I regret what I did. I think now, like before, things will really get bad and I need to get out of the market again before they get any worse."

What she ended up experiencing is called the whipsaw effect. It's when someone repeatedly endures only one side of the volatility, the downside, without benefiting from the inevitable upside. This is why most people with knowledge of the stock market know that market downturns are temporary.

A key feature of this principle is that you must be on the right course to begin with. If you own ill-conceived investments you don't understand, they could be exactly the wrong kinds of stocks to have going into an economic or market downturn. The advice we provided that would have worked for this lady didn't help her because she ignored it. Over the next seven years she had a small number of investment successes but a much higher number of investment failures. It wasn't because the stocks she had chosen were bad. The losses she suffered happened each time she got this feeling in her bones, decided it justified getting out of the market and later thought she would somehow know when to get back in.

It turned out that her "feelings" about when to take her money out amounted to the most accurate predictor of short-term stock market fluctuations we had ever seen. The problem was that when she thought it was time to get out, it was almost always the best time to get in.

The lady lost approximately half of the $50,000 she was investing after four years. We were concurrently handling the larger chunk of her money. The $200,000 we were investing grew to about $250,000 during the same period, and this was through the tough times after the collapse of the tech bubble, the scandals involving Enron and Wall Street, and the September 11, 2001, terrorist attacks.

This client might have been an extreme example. But we can point to dozens of similar clients who allowed us to manage the entireties of their portfolios, but still regularly called and voiced their opinions and fears when the markets fluctuated and wavered, requiring emotional handholding. Such behavior is very normal; dealing with it and reassuring investors they are doing the right thing is part of the job of any conscientious and responsible financial advisor.

Almost everybody, including most professional advisors, get upset stomachs when the going gets rough. The key is becoming detached from emotional decision-making (that feeling in your bones) and remaining committed to a plan that was conceived using informed and rational logic free from the craziness of the moment.

That's exactly what FlexScore does for you: It removes the

emotion that comes with the ups and downs of the investment markets, and replaces it with the genuine gratification of seeing your score improve because you are taking actions that are within your control.

Take a look at the following table contrasting two different investment strategies. Let's say you had $100,000 to invest. Using the set of return percentages in the first column below featuring a higher-risk investment portfolio (ranging from the high of a 21 percent return in the second year to a low of a 16 percent loss in the fourth year), your $100,000 would turn into $147,000 at the end of the five year period covered by the table. You might be surprised to know that if you chose the scenario in the second column reflecting a more moderate-risk investment portfolio (a steady 8 percent return in each of the five years), your initial $100,000 would also turn into the same $147,000.

Year	(+) or (-)	(+) or (-)
1	+20%	+8%
2	+21%	+8%
3	+10%	+8%
4	-16%	+8%
5	+10%	+8%

(Source: Investment managers Atalanta Sosnoff and Eagle Asset Management.)

The real question you need to ask yourself is did you assume that the first column of returns would give you a higher return than the second column? If you did and had chosen that type of higher-risk portfolio, then you would have needed to make sure you had the fortitude and stomach to stay the course through all five years of market ups and downs. Many people give lip service to the idea that they have a high-risk tolerance. However, when they suffer a decent loss in their portfolio, many who claim they can handle the risks somehow "chicken out" and decide to change their investment course. Those who, after the fourth year

16 percent loss in value decided to become more conservative by selling out and transferring their investments to cash would not have benefited from year five's positive return of 10 percent. They would have been left with $133,363, instead of $147,000. Although such growth in their original $100,000 would have been nothing to scoff at, the annualized return over five years would have only been 4.9 percent. Remember, if they would have just stuck with it, they would have earned 8 percent annually. The second column of consistent returns would have returned the same 8 percent annualized. However, there is a big difference between the two potential results.

What's the lesson? Having a high-risk tolerance, whether it's a true tolerance or you just wish it is so, means you still have to stay the course and not change paths in the middle of your long-term plan. The only valid reason to make all-encompassing changes in the amount of risk you're willing to take on is if your financial circumstances change. Examples would include if you or an income-producing spouse become permanently disabled or if you inherit a windfall amount of cash. But outside of potential major life events such as these, truly knowing your investment personality and sticking to its respective path is tantamount to realizing investment success.

We're investment professionals with much experience under our belts. But even we don't have direct insight into the future or a magical crystal ball. (We did, but it broke.) We still have to operate within the same parameters everybody else has at their disposal. We suffered like everybody else through the post-2008 market downturn.

Remember our client with the $1 million who gave us half to invest while he invested the other half? Although his portfolio went on the decline for a while in 2008, today he still has more than $1 million. Both he and we are 100 percent convinced that if he had been left to his own devices and invested his entire $1 million using his methodologies, he would have much less today. The moral of the story isn't that we're such geniuses. It's that with realistic expectations and a well thought out methodology, success can be attained given enough time, patience and commitment.

There are plenty of people who think the world of investment is one in which the biggest risk you face is losing all of your money in the stock market. This is of course a possibility, but the probability of it happening is very slim so long as you adopt a diversified investment approach.

The biggest risk, as illustrated in the stories we've presented, is when after losing a large chunk of your portfolio, even if it is only temporary, you allow it to impair your ability to do well in the future as a result of the ingenious phenomenon called compounding.

Albert Einstein said, "Compounding interest is the eighth wonder of the world. He who understands it earns it…He who doesn't pays it."

Compounding is essentially earning interest or a rate of return on money you've already earned as interest. If you have $100,000, and earn a 5 percent return in one year, you start your second year at $105,000. So if you earn another five percent annual return, you don't just earn $5,000 in the second year; you earn a little bit more because you also earn interest on the $5,000 you earned the first year.

Now think of it in a negative way: If you suffer a $5,000 loss, you've impaired your ability to compound money because for every percentage point you lost, you need to make up that much and then some just to get back to even.

As you march forward on your way to becoming financially independent, it is extremely important to always remember the amount of money you have working for you should be moving higher rather than lower at all times. If it moves lower you decrease the odds of benefiting from the process of compounding.

There are myriad examples of people who came to us as

clients after having lost a relatively large amount of money in the stock market and insisted, "We'll never invest in the stock market again." It was as if the stock market had it out for them. We can understand the emotional pain of being burned by the proverbial flame and not being anxious to get burned again. However, hiding yourself away in a deep silo to avoid any and all forms of investment risk only exposes you to one of the largest and most prevalent risks any person can face: longevity.

Many people approach us wanting to retire and ask our counsel about how much they can spend and never run out of money, meaning the principal that produces the income they plan to live on for the rest of their lives. We reply, somewhat tongue-in-cheek. "Perfect, we'll come up with that calculation as soon as you tell us the date you're going to die."

They inevitably stare back at us with a look of shock on their faces as if they should have an answer. Normally, we don't know the precise day we'll leave this earth. Because of that reality we all have to plan on living a life that's going to be a little bit longer than we might anticipate. By shielding yourself from investment risk, for good or bad reasons, you inevitably increase the odds you won't make enough return on your investments to last you the entirety of your life.

A married couple in their mid-60s has a greater than 50 percent chance of one spouse living into his or her 90s given today's state of medical science. If you continually focus on potentially losing your money in the investment markets, you underestimate the larger risk of running out of money before you run out of life. After all, financial independence is a place we all want to reach, where money and the stress that comes from not having enough of it are the least of our worries.

No one can predict with much accuracy how long he or she will live. Yes, you can examine genetics: "My family doesn't live very long," you might conclude. But that's only one factor. Others include living a healthier lifestyle than your ancestors, the wonders of modern medicine or improvements in environmental and workforce protections. There was little to be done to affect longevity in our grandparents' or even our parents' days. There was little to be done about heart disease then. Today a lot can be done.

Jeff's father died at the age of 48, after having his second heart attack in a year. He was a Type A personality, held a high-stress sales job, drank and smoked too much, ate all the wrong things and never exercised. He was the epitome of how not to take care of yourself. If all Jeff has to rely upon are his genetics, he might also plan on dying in his late 40s. But genetics is only one piece of the pie. Lifespan also has a lot to do with behavior. It's like financial planning: The things you can control through your behavior are just as important, if not more so, than the things you can't control.

You can control how well you invest in the markets and how much you contribute to those investments every month. The rest has to be left up to forces that are much larger than anyone can manage.

So before you embark upon your journey towards financial independence, it is imperative to honestly understand your investment behavior and risk tolerance. That way you can achieve those consistent rates of return without giving up when the going gets rough, which happens from time to time. It doesn't matter whether you invest in stocks, mutual funds, bonds, precious metals, real estate or any other medium. There is no such thing as an investment that does well 100 percent of the time. Also remember that the risk of longevity in today's modern world is still the biggest financial risk we all face.

We've spent much of this chapter talking about the investment markets and the fact that they matter because we know they are the No. 1 topic our clients, and most American investors, are preoccupied with. If the biggest risk we face is longevity, something we can't control, and the biggest risk most Americans focus on when it comes to their financial affairs is the investment market, something they also think they can't control, then there must be things over which they *can* exercise control.

One reason FlexScore is such a valuable tool is that it takes away the concentration from the investment markets and properly places it on those items of financial necessity you can control. FlexScore is the way to quantify how well you are doing on all the many things you can control in your financial life.

A young couple with small children has a set of risks that are different than an older couple with grown children. Typically, the younger a couple is, the fewer assets they possess. The biggest thing the younger couple has going for it is the earnings potential over time of two working spouses. The possibility of dying young is so often overlooked at that age. It's not a high probability, but if it does occur, the consequences can be devastating for the family and surviving minor children; so dire is that eventuality that steps need to be taken to guard against the risk such as obtaining appropriate insurance. There are many insurance options from which to choose, but the fact of the matter is that young people don't have to spend a whole lot of money to adequately protect their families.

The older couple with adult children living outside the home confronts a different kind of risk. They may have a decent amount of assets in the ideal situation. They need to consider some of the same risks as the younger couple such as dying prematurely. They also need to adequately protect themselves and their assets such as home equity and a nest egg against unforeseen events that could set them back such as uninsured losses, lawsuits or early death. They need different kinds of insurance products.

People of pre-retirement age, in their mid-50s, may see surviving parents requiring some kind of assistance or convalescent care. They may feel a certain sense of moral duty, witnessing their once strong and vital parents experiencing old age. That's when these 50-something-year-olds may also consider purchasing long-term care insurance policies for themselves that would pay for the costs of caretakers, either at home or in a care facility, without depleting the nest eggs they have worked so hard to build up.

We all face risks in our own times. This isn't to say the young couple just starting out and having children shouldn't protect their assets or property. It's just that their focus may be on one risk rather than another.

These diversities of focus and need are precisely why FlexScore is so invaluable. The score rates you based on your unique financial situation and objectives. They may not be the same situation and objectives as your neighbor, even if he or she is of a like age and circumstance. That's why everyone's FlexScore is different, even if they make the same income and claim the same assets; income and assets are only two elements of a multi-component equation.

We bring up people's fallacies about investment and risk not just because they are all too common, but to make the point that consistency is the key to success with investing and, frankly, all financial success. Consistency counts more than anything else. It is important to earn a consistent rate of return on your investments. It's important to consistently save so you have the wherewithal to invest. It is important to get yourself out of debt and stay there so you can put yourself on the path of growing your money instead of constantly wasting your income by paying back other people for using their money. Consistency moves you towards financial independence faster than any other factor.

There's nothing exotic or sexy about it. People think you have to become some sort of slick, fast-talking financial guru to know how to be financially independent. It's all about steady behavior and not about inside knowledge or mysterious schemes. We all remember from childhood Aesop's fable about "The Tortoise and the Hare," the story of a race between two mismatched contestants and how the slow but plodding tortoise defeats the swift yet overconfident hare. Consistency and steadiness are the formula for success in financial planning as well as in athletic competition.

A common affliction we encounter is among clients who by many measures have made it, at least for the near term. They have achieved a measure of financial success, often because of their careers or businesses. But past success doesn't necessarily translate into success in the long term. Still, these clients frequently come to think they know it all and aren't open to advice. They are also frequently unwilling to accept change or consider taking less risk with their money.

Recency bias is a symptom of this affliction. This is a tendency by most people to place a higher value on events that occurred most recently in the past versus events that have taken place over a longer period of time. In other words, it's the human mind replacing the law of averages with an alternative though fanciful world we can more easily, and comfortably, understand.

A well-established psychological phenomenon that affects many people making financial and especially investment decisions, recency bias is part of an arena called behavioral finance. Michael Pompian is one of the best financial authors who have written on the topic. Here's how he describes the issue in his 2012 book *Behavioral Finance and Investor Types: Managing Behavior to Make Better Investment Decisions*:

> Followers [of recency bias] tend to be dissociated from the investing process, preferring instead to take an easier route to making investment decisions by either following the crowd (investing in whatever the mass audience is doing) or by following the advice of friends and colleagues. Recency bias occurs when investors look at the most recent performance of an investment and make a decision to invest based on that most recent performance. This is a very common behavior....

Does Pompian's explanation sound familiar?

Take this example. Jason flew out of Hartford, Connecticut bound for Sacramento, California on September 14, 2001, three days after 9-11, when terrorists hijacked airlines and flew them into the Twin Towers, a field in Pennsylvania and the Pentagon. The whole nation was suffering from a form of PTSD (posttraumatic stress disorder) when it came to commercial air travel. They evacuated the entire airport terminal before Jason's flight was allowed to board, and that was after all passengers went through security. Every piece of baggage was inspected, piece-by-piece. Bomb-sniffing dogs inspected the plane before passengers were let on. There were only 14 passengers on this large airliner because people were afraid to fly.

It wasn't that people should have felt comfortable flying following such monstrous tragedies. But in reality, this was the safest time to fly in the history of the nation up until that time, even in comparison to the much more stringent and technologically advanced security precautions in place today.

Getting back to investing and financial markets, around the same time, in the year 2000, many people approached us asking whether they could do better with their money, seeking investment returns of 15 percent or higher. Their expectations were based on the just-passed decade of the 1990s, in the wake of the dot.com boom when investors expected such high returns as a matter of course. As we now know, this was just before the "dot.com" bust that started to hit in late 2000.

People were mistakenly basing their investment decisions on what had most recently occurred (a booming market fueled by the mushrooming value of high-tech stocks) instead of letting the law of averages guide their reasoning. The law of averages says over a long period of time the probability of an event happening at a higher than average rate will more than likely be offset by a time period during which a lower rate of occurrence will prevail. Just because investments are returning very well over a short period of time doesn't mean this is a new normal. It is probably a temporary upside that will likely be replaced eventually by the flipside: A temporary below average rate of return.

Averaging out the results, you end up getting exactly what a logical person would expect: Things will in all likelihood ultimately even themselves out. That isn't to say that the human mind isn't immune to decisions based on rash emotion.

In late 2012, right after the general election, the nation was preoccupied by the impending "fiscal cliff" and dire negative economic and financial predictions of tax hikes and spending cuts automatically taking effect on January 1, 2013, unless Congress and the President acted. We were out of town at a financial industry conference in Chicago. Dire warnings of this fiscal cliff hit the national news. They were featured on all the cable and network news shows and financial programs, and on innumerable Internet sites. We received a bunch of calls from worried clients asking us whether they should pull out of the stock market or otherwise change their investment behavior based on these warnings.

"We've made sound decisions based on the long term," we responded. "If knee-jerk reactions are what you use to make long-term decisions, you'll very likely never achieve any of your financial goals." Short-term happenings almost always make the uninitiated feel they are the definition of the new normal over the long term. They usually aren't. There are any number of stocks that experience a very good one, two or three year time frame when their prices shoot up far above average. That convinces any number of people to give up their investments in long-term companies offering more stable return rates and instead place their money in stocks that seem to be going up more quickly. That is precisely the time not to do so. If we adopt a long-term approach and see that an investment has recently gone up quite a lot, that may be a good time to move away from that stock and protect your capital rather than assume this remarkable, recent record of performance will continue into the future. Too often it doesn't.

A more mundane example of this phenomenon explains why a lot of people don't get life insurance. Unless you've recently had a close call with death, which most people don't, you might say, "Yeah, I should probably consider life insurance, but I've been okay in the past and will probably be fine into the future, so I won't buy that insurance." Plenty of people who should have insurance convince themselves that they'll never need it. On the other hand, people who recently experienced the passing of a friend or family member will sometimes over-insure themselves.

Another common behavioral bias negatively affecting people's finances is overconfidence. For example, another of our clients was an overconfident executive of a big local bank. He retired with $2 million worth of his bank stock and visited an advisor at a major brokerage firm, where he was advised to sell half of his bank stock and use the money to diversify his holdings. The Wall Street advisor also recommended he divest himself of the remaining $1 million so as to spread out his tax burden over four years instead of assuming it all at once.

The Wall Street firm's advisor was offering good advice and following sound practices. The client should have followed the advice but didn't because it was a much more conservative approach than he had been using.

After four years the investments hadn't gone anywhere, neither up nor down in value. By the late 1990s our executive turned to another Wall Street brokerage firm and obtained similar advice: Liquidate his bank stock and put his money into diversified investments. By this time the dot.com high-tech stocks were booming. Some of his friends were making returns of 80 or 100 percent a year. The executive was eager to cash in, too.

The second Wall Street company was heavily into high-tech investments. The executive had finally found an advisor who told him what he wanted to hear: He could double his money. The new advisor put charts in front of him showing that his money would have doubled in the past year if he had bought dot.com stocks. Our executive couldn't wait to take the advice.

He sold $1.5 million of his $2 million in stock, paid the taxes and some leftover debt; he still held onto about $500,000 in bank stock. He was left with $1 million to invest in 1999. He bought high-tech stocks in early 2000. Unfortunately, by March 2002, he was left with just $330,000 out of the $1 million he held before. The executive had bought the dot.com stocks just in time to see them plummet in value in what is now called the "dot.com bust" that started in 2000. Our guy's timing was terrible.

The executive lamented that he was a ship stuck out at sea without a rudder. He didn't know what to do. He contemplated going back to work because he no longer had the financial horsepower he once did. After floundering for a few years, he turned to us in 2007, with total assets of roughly $800,000 (his $500,000 in bank stock and the $330,000 that survived the dot. com bust). He informed us his expectation was to make a 15 percent rate of return on the investments we would make for him.

Just like the advisors from the two Wall Street firms, we advised him to sell the balance of the bank stocks and invest his money in a well-diversified portfolio, including much more than just high-tech stocks. He was never willing to accept our advice. He did hand over to us the $330,000 left over from his tech stocks. We managed that money the way we invest, putting it into a diversified portfolio that produced a more moderate 9 percent rate of return over time and with far less risk than what he had been taking. Our client continued holding onto his bank stock, and still does to this day. The problem was that the economic crisis of 2008 arrived and the stock market tanked, especially for financial and bank-related companies. The executive lost much of his money that was invested in the bank stock.

This guy had a Dr. Jekyll and Mr. Hyde personality. He started out expecting a 15 percent return rate. But when the market suffered a temporary sell off and went down, he wanted to pull out of the investment portfolio we created for him and funnel his money into certificates of deposit, which at the time had interest rates in the low single digits. You couldn't get much more than 1 percent interest then. We talked our client out of going into CDs and into riding out the storm instead.

The stock market performed as it usually does. It was down in 2008, but went up dramatically in 2009, and continued to move up in 2010. Our guy had still averaged a return of 9 percent a year through the year 2010, despite the 2008 economic downturn. But during a client review meeting he said his investments weren't producing enough of a return. He once again expressed his desire for a 15 percent annual return although he was still fearful of the volatility in market value that a strategy seeking 15 percent a year can produce.

Meanwhile, his bank stocks, which he was still controlling, were achieving little more than a 2 percent increase in value during the three years after he first came to us. We, on the other hand, were achieving a 9 percent rate of return on that portion of his investments we managed. In the face of his demand for a 15 percent return rate, we agreed to disagree and parted ways. He decided to manage his money on his own. The last thing he told us about was a feeling he had that the stock market was going to go down again and he was once more considering putting everything into CDs. Since then, the market has continued going up.

This guy's overconfidence came from his past career as a successful executive. Like the doctors we discussed earlier and others who exhibit a great deal of investment confidence, their certainty comes from the experience in their respective fields and not from legitimate experience with investments and markets.

The message here is that overconfidence can cause under-performance in your financial life. Also, don't seek help by searching for advisors who will be your "yes" men or women. They won't compliment your weaknesses; they'll only exacerbate them.

A retired man and wife in their 60s were also among our clients. The man had worked in a large company's information technology department. His wife was a stay-at-home mom. They made all of their financial decisions together.

Their friends who were longtime clients of ours referred this couple. The referring couple initially gave us complete control and discretion over their money and were always satisfied with how we handled their assets and provided them with a monthly income stream from the proceeds of their investments.

The new couple had no pension. The only guaranteed retirement income they would receive was Social Security, but at the time they came to us they were too young to qualify for payments. They did have $1 million, a combination of his 401(k) account and some money they had realized from the sale of real estate property.

Our new clients had no financial background and they were their own worst enemy. They began to read articles on the Internet with doomsday accounts predicting everything in the world was going to come to an end, that the financial systems were broken, that the markets couldn't be trusted and that retail investors such as themselves never made any money; only the large institutions saw returns. They believed the financial services industry was manipulating the stock market only for the benefit of the industry and that the smaller investor was always the victim.

During the normal course of events, their $1 million portfolio might temporarily go down in value by $30,000 or $40,000. They would panic. They'd call us with instructions to pivot from a moderately aggressive type of investment strategy to a more conservative approach because in their mind the market was about to implode. Because of the danger of getting whipsawed, their attitude was not a good thing. As we mentioned in ealier chapters, getting whipsawed is when the fear some investors feel becomes so great that they turn from a moderate-aggressive to a conservative-oriented portfolio to avoid volatility in the markets in the hope their money won't go down any further. However, when the market bounces back, as it always has, the whipsawed investors have locked themselves into the losses they've already suffered and are unable to take advantage of a market upturn.

Moderate-aggressive investors know the stock market will go up and down. But if they set a five-year or longer horizon for their investments, the reward should be far greater if they are invested moderately-aggressively than conservatively. Those who maintain a moderate-aggressive portfolio in diversified investments have always fared better by staying fully invested over time and by not allowing the emotional roller coaster of the market to dictate their investment style and strategy.

This couple that were our clients got whipsawed. Their portfolio went down a little, filling them with alarm and prompting them to adopt a conservative portfolio in early 2007. Then, when the stock market quickly rebounded, they missed the "up" cycle. They felt bad about doing this to themselves and decided to get back into the market in a moderate-aggressive mode in March 2008, just in time for the big market downturn that hit the entire nation. By the end of that year they had lost 20 percent of their money and panicked even more. Again against our advice, they once more turned to a conservative portfolio. The market swung back significantly in 2009, went up quite a lot and continued to do so. Had our couple stayed the course, within a year or two they would have recovered what they lost in 2008, and realized a decent rate of return in the following years.

Instead, they allowed themselves to be whipsawed for the second time in two years. So rather than temporarily losing some money but gaining it back and even growing their investments by navigating a steady course in the market they permanently lost part of their capital. The couple continued to feel frustrated and upset, convinced they were about to lose all of their money. They allowed their fear to dominate their behavior. Their $1 million initial nest egg is worth $800,000 today. They still can't acknowledge the mistakes they committed. They blame the market and not themselves, which is an easy way to swallow their pride. In reality, it was their decisions to change their risk profile multiple times amid changing market conditions, and not the market, that caused them to lose $200,000. It all leads back to recency bias and the whipsaw affect.

Still another example of what not to do can be seen in the case of a building contractor client who came to us in 2006. At age 50, he was a self-made millionaire who began building his business from nothing and turned it into $25 million in assets in less than 10 years. We had worked with his company and its employees since 2001, providing counseling services in connection with the firm's retirement plan. We met with the owner and his chief financial officer, his CPA and his banker in a private room at a high-end restaurant to discuss how to protect some of his $25 million in net worth.

We learned during the meeting that 100 percent of his net worth was tied up in the one thing that created it: His successful business. Like most successful entrepreneurs, it was difficult for our client to think about diverting money out of his thriving business into assets that had not grown nearly as fast. Like other business owners who do well financially because of their businesses, he ended up becoming attached to it as if it was an offspring. He had spent so much time with his business, made his decisions based on what was in the company's best interest, guided it and was proud of it. The success of his business also represented security for his family and the employees he cared about.

Such people feel they can't turn their backs on the business and never consider that continuing to invest all or most of their assets in the business poses serious potential risks. The wisdom of diversifying or taking some money out of the company and putting it somewhere else for future financial security escapes them. At best, they may consider using money from the company as seed capital to start another related business, which amounts to diversification, but not in an ideal way.

We recommended that our client take $5 million of his $25 million out of the company, pay off his home mortgage of $1 million, invest $1 million in an equity or stock portfolio, put another $1 million into municipal bonds, invest $1 million in alternative assets such as oil, precious metals, currency, commodities and real estate, and hold onto the remaining $1 million as cash in the form of CDs for a rainy day. Keeping the last $1 million liquid meant he could get his hands on it immediately if it became necessary.

The client decided he would place $1 million of his money into State of California municipal bonds, but didn't take any of our other advice. He then proceeded to borrow against the $1 million in municipal bonds so his company could buy more equipment. The bank used the municipal bond portfolio as collateral on the loan they made to his business.

Our client's construction company tanked in 2008, succumbing to the Great Recession. It had begun a number of major projects that couldn't be completed because his customers' financing dried up. His company's lines of credit dried up too.

The bank called back all of his notes and lines of credit. Since consumers couldn't pay him the money he was owed for the projects his company was working on, he couldn't pay back the bank. His finances were highly leveraged because he had borrowed so much money against his assets in order to fuel the growth of his business. He paid $7 million for the building that housed his company. Overnight, it was now worth $4 million and he still owed $5 million on it to the bank. The same thing happened to all of his other assets.

Since he didn't have the money the bank was demanding, our client literally lost everything: His company, his $1 million in municipal bonds that was being used as collateral on loans, his home and 100 percent of his personal assets. He ended up bankrupt.

If the guy had followed our advice and diversified his resources only two years earlier, he would have taken much of his personal risk off the table. His family would not have to some extent been entirely dependent on his business' ability to make money. It was far riskier for him to keep 100 percent of his wealth in his construction company versus using some of the profits to buy different assets, whether they were stocks, bonds or real estate. If he had done that, his company might have been able to withstand the economic tumult and still exist today. At least he would have preserved his home and much of his personal assets, which were substantial.

Because he was convinced that the business that created all this wealth in the first place was the best place to invest 100 percent of his money, today he's flat broke. He didn't see the economic downturn coming and he was totally unprepared to manage his way through it.

What's brilliant about FlexScore is that it awards points to you for doing the right things and takes points away for doing the wrong things. If the people in the examples we cited in this chapter had been using FlexScore, they would have seen the logic in our recommendations, only they would have arrived at the same conclusions on their own, instead of simply taking our word for it. FlexScore would have empirically and objectively demonstrated to them how the bad decisions they were contemplating would negatively impact other key aspects of their financial lives.

We often ask our clients who present us with illogical financial ideas, "Would you advise your good friends to take this course you're proposing if they faced the same financial circumstances you face?" When they really give it careful thought, most of them answer, "No, we wouldn't."

Then we ask, "If you're looking at things from an objective point of view, how can you advise your friends not to do something you're prepared to do for yourself?"

The operative phrase is "objective point of view." FlexScore allows you to arrive at that objective point of view on your own... objectively. You can see it with your own eyes. And you can see exactly how your decisions will potentially impact other pieces of your financial life.

CHAPTER EIGHT

What Does It Mean If Your Score Sucks?

"The bad news is time flies.
The good news is you're the pilot."

—Michael Althsuler, inspirational speaker and author

Let's just admit that there will be plenty of people who will end up with a relatively low FlexScore when they start out. That high probability means the sinking feeling in their gut that they haven't been doing the right things financially all these years may well be justified. This chapter is about what they, and you, can do to improve your score if it isn't satisfactory.

If you ended up getting a "D" in a college course, it was probably a direct reflection of your effort or lack thereof. What happened? You didn't pay attention? You didn't apply yourself? You didn't study? You can probably retake the class in the hopes of earning a better grade, although that isn't always guaranteed.

If your FlexScore is low, what can *you* do to improve it? What if there are things you can't improve given the amount of time you have left before you are hoping to reach your goals? Then what do you do? Can you restart your financial life? Can you go back and redo what you've done or haven't done over a period of decades? If there are few opportunities remaining in the future in order to fix the past, what can you do now to improve the outcome? These are some of the questions we aim to address in this chapter.

There are two things against which you can be compared. First, there are your peers. What happens if your FlexScore isn't as good as your friends, your family, your colleagues or your neighbors, the people who are comparable to you in income and lifestyle? Although such a test may be the best way to keep up with the Joneses, it is likely not correct or helpful to compare yourself to someone else. We believe providing you with information about how you compare to your peers can be used as an inherent motivator for you. But the magic of FlexScore derives from its ability to present you with a score in relation to the goals and objectives you've carefully identified for yourself. Therefore, the best way to know if your score sucks is to examine your goals and objectives first and foremost, not someone else's. If you have a low score and you're approaching the period of time when you would like to achieve financial independence, it means the clock is ticking and you are losing opportunities to raise your score.

This is a good moment to review the components that make up the maximum of 1,000 points it is possible to earn with FlexScore.

The first 500 points you can achieve come from observing the financial fundamentals that we call "building the nest." They encompass getting your financial house in order, making sure you spend less than you make and ensuring that your loved ones will be okay if something bad happens to you.

If your score is low because of deficiencies in this area, you are facing some financial problems and confront risks against which you are not protected. But if the wind blows in your direction and lady luck comes your way, you may still make it to, and through, retirement without hitting any huge bumps in the road. If some changes are made, you might still live a long and healthy financial life.

The second portion of the FlexScore is where you can earn up to 500 points by what we term "funding the nest." Remember, this involves putting an appropriate amount of money away each month to fund the goals you've fashioned for yourself, which includes retirement. It embraces investing your money with the correct amount of risk you are prepared to tolerate. It means not taking on too much debt and, if necessary, reducing or eliminating the debt you already have. And it's focusing on the portion of your nest egg that will provide your future income so that it's flexible, liquid and available to you at an earlier time if you should need to draw upon it.

If your score is failing in this area, there really is no easy way to fix it other than through your concentrated efforts in the time you have remaining. As we've repeatedly mentioned in this book, the biggest risk we all face is running out of money before running out of life. A low score in this second half of FlexScore means the risk for you is high.

If your score is well below 1,000 (the score we deem to be as close as possible to perfect) and you are nearing the age at which you had hoped to accomplish financial independence, then you can forget about the stock and real estate markets. Because assuming you will live a long life, your chances of running out of money before you run out of life are great. And no matter how well or badly those markets perform, you're probably not going to make it to your stated goal anyway.

If you are now 60 years old and presently live a lifestyle that would require a $2 million investment portfolio to maintain, and all you've saved is $200,000, there's no possible way for you to accumulate the additional $1.8 million it would take to preserve your current style of living by a typical retirement age of, say 65. You are guaranteed to run out of money before you run out of life if you live that life in retirement the same way you did in pre-retirement.

It is important to remember that FlexScore is only a snapshot in time, an objective and realistic picture; but it isn't a life sentence.

There are basically three options with which you can respond if you have deficiencies in the bottom section of FlexScore:

1. Work later in life than you had planned.

2. Adjust downward the amount of money you need with which to retire.

3. Hope you don't live as long as the average American.

The key ingredient in all three alternatives is being willing to change. Let's take a look at your options for change in both areas of FlexScore.

FlexScore's first 500 points

Perhaps you've set too many goals for yourself or too lofty of a goal. Retiring to a better lifestyle than you lead today may be a nice notion, but it also may not be a reasonable expectation. We earlier related the story of an immigrant blue-collar woman laboring at a tomato processing plant who lived a very modest lifestyle but through diligence and discipline built up a nest egg of $400,000, and still has some years of her working life ahead of her to further build her savings. She will likely be able to live better in retirement than she does now, if she desires. Plus, she will be able to offer her children opportunities she didn't have.

The situation of this working woman will rarely be the case with most people. It's not impossible, but most people lack the discipline, patience and self-sacrifice to accomplish what our retirement plan participant built up with a modest income. Too often people have this idyllic notion about retirement: That it will be filled with exotic and more frequent travel and purchases that they've never made before; that it will introduce a lifestyle they haven't yet experienced. Remember when we said that money can buy you experiences but it doesn't necessarily mean your life will be better? If you enjoyed a decent life while working, why should you expect a better life in retirement?

One way to think of the future is to ask yourself: If tomorrow I could magically know I was going to receive a lump sum of money once a month that fulfilled all of my living needs and satisfied my current lifestyle without my having to work, would that make it worthwhile to look forward to retirement? Fulfilling that goal doesn't require having more money than you live on now; it just frees you from the burden of putting in a full day's work every day.

Another mistake we see a great deal is couples with minor children wanting to pay for their kids' entire college education. That is frequently a lofty goal, which can also be unrealistic with today's inflated college expenses. If helping your children pay all of their college costs seriously detracts from your ultimate ability to retire, it becomes a detriment to your financial future. Ironically, the end result could be compelling your children to some day care for you, if they have the ability, because you haven't properly planned for yourself. If this happens, we hope your children don't follow in your financial footsteps and that the apple *does* fall far from the tree.

What's wrong with your kids qualifying for grants, scholarships or loans to finance their higher education? This is one place where going into debt can be a wise choice because they're creating the debt to invest in themselves and boost their lifetime earning capacity. Unlike college, you as parents can't apply for grants, scholarships or loans to fund your retirement. The bottom line: In this case you have to put your welfare ahead of your children's. Paying for your kids' entire education is a noble goal, but not always possible. They may be better off learning how to take care of themselves on this count anyway.

Even though we're talking about the first 500 points in FlexScore, building the nest, it is related to how well you've done and the state of your capacity on the second 500 points, which is funding the nest from this time forward. If you make $30,000 a year now, you shouldn't have a dream of parlaying that income into the lifestyle of a millionaire during retirement. We need to set realistic expectations for ourselves and for our ability to fund those expectations based on our earning capacity while we're working. The biggest risk in dealing with the first 500 points in FlexScore is when your eyes are bigger than your stomach. It is a real drag in reaching your goals if they are based on accumulating an amount of money you are incapable of achieving.

There's nothing magical about improving your score on the first 500 points. It can be done. It's like waking up and having a messy house. You can awake and bemoan having a messy house or you can put your nose to the grindstone and clean it up.

For example, improving the initial 500 points in FlexScore gets accomplished by making sure you have the proper protections in place when it comes to life, disability and long term care insurance. FlexScore helps people calculate the appropriate amount of insurance they need in these categories depending on their individual needs and family situations. If you are underinsured, the best way to fix that discrepancy is to get properly insured; then your points will go up. Let's say you're married with minor children and you and your spouse have talked with each other about what would happen if the both of you were to die, but you've never communicated your wishes in the form of a simple will or guardianship paperwork. Those legal documents need to be created. It's not a big deal. Then your point score will improve.

If every year at tax time you find yourself having to pay a lot more in taxes than you expected and this is an ongoing issue, you need to get your tax planning under control and either find a way to earn more deductions or take better advantage of the existing tax code so ideally at the end of the tax year you don't have to pay a lot more or get a lot back. As in the fable Goldilocks and the Three Bears, when it comes to the amount of taxes you should pay, the amount should be "just right," not too much and not too little.

Finally, when it comes to monthly cash flow, you need to be

certain that you're not spending more than you take in between the 1ˢᵗ and the 30ᵗʰ of each month. On one hand, this is pretty elementary and one of the easier things to fix. On the other hand, it can be difficult because it might require altering some ingrained behaviors about which you may not even be aware.

If your problems with a low FlexScore reside in the first 500 points, building the nest, the good news is that with some relatively small adjustments you can get on track.

FlexScore's second 500 points

The reality isn't as simple if your problems from a low FlexScore rest with the last 500 points, funding the nest. Fixing these dilemmas is more complicated and potentially problematic. So let's look at the problems involving the major categories making up funding the nest, what you need to acknowledge in terms of identifying the problems and what, if anything, you can do about them.

1. Your nest egg investments are inflexible or illiquid (what we describe as asset liquidity in Chapter Three).

You can be a millionaire and not have any cash or ability to spend much of your money. This is counterproductive. You've heard the term house rich, cash poor? Here's a real-life example: Early in Jeff's career, he met a construction worker who was looking for some financial planning help. He had inherited two homes in the San Francisco Bay Area. The worker was "instantly" wealthy because each home was worth nearly $2 million. But he had no easy ability to turn those houses into cash. Sure, he could find renters, but the amount of monthly rental income earned would be low compared to what he might be able to realize if he had access to the entire cash value of the home. However, he couldn't sell the properties because his inheritance was restricted by the way the houses were held in trust. So he was a multi-millionaire but didn't have any money.

Another client who was worth tens of millions of dollars

knew this phenomenon well. With the unoccupied properties she owned, she was worth a whole bunch of money on paper. But that paper didn't generate scratch at the end of the month, such as cash to pay bills and living expenses plus give her a little walking around money in her purse. What good is being worth a lot of money? Just because you have a lot of assets doesn't mean you have a lot of cash to spend.

This dilemma describes the plight of many farmers in the Central Valley of California. They can be worth more than $1 million because they are rich in owning some of the most productive farming land in the world. That doesn't necessarily equate to cash in the pocket.

This is what we mean by possessing illiquid assets. It is a problem experienced by a lot of ordinary people who aren't multi-millionaires or big growers.

A similar dilemma comes when people do financial planning and include the equity in their homes among their assets. Having equity in your house makes you feel better; it makes you seem richer. The problem when doing financial planning and listing the equity in your home as an asset is this: You need to have a place to lay your head at night. Your home is shelter, not an investment. Your home equity provides you with a safety net; if you have a financial emergency you can sell that home or use it to qualify for a home equity line of credit. But that's only a last resort. Your home shouldn't be considered when you're talking about investments.

Yes, you could be worth $1 million if it includes the home you live in. But how do you convert that $1 million home into liquidity or cash flow? Short of selling it, there is no way. And the average person is not going to do that voluntarily because he or she likes the home and is emotionally and financially invested in the house.

Owning a liquid asset is a different story. It provides you with flexibility. You don't have to sell your home in order to get cash out. You can sell a few hundred shares of stock or a portion of a mutual fund. You can take money out of your savings account or CD. You can cash out some value in your whole life insurance policy. You can maybe even live on the interest your liquid portfolio generates and not have to sell anything.

If you own 1,000 shares of General Electric stock and need cash right away, that asset can be instantly sold and cash will immediately be made available. If you own illiquid assets such as property, a business, collectibles, certain long-term annuities, then the same option is not available.

Even real estate, a valid investment for many, is not so simple If you want to sell real property, you have to find a real estate agent, establish its value, list the property, show the property, hope someone makes a reasonable offer, negotiate the terms of the sales contract and pray the buyer quickly qualifies for a mortgage and is able to close the escrow. This is a complicated, time consuming process. If you need the money today, forget it; it's not possible.

Agricultural property is another example of illiquid assets with which we have had experience. It's different from residential real estate. These are larger properties. There are fewer interested buyers. And the sales process is more involved. If you own 1,000 acres of pastureland, you have to find someone looking to buy 1,000 acres of pastureland. Everyone needs a house in which to live. Not everyone needs 1,000 acres of pastureland. There are very few people who do. The more unique the property, the fewer potential buyers there are out there.

Many people base their calculation of net worth on the businesses they own and operate. Here is what they frequently overlook: If you own a business, its value is often contingent on the state of your health and your willingness to be there to make sure it's running properly on a day-to-day basis. Few small or medium-sized businesses can prosper as fruitfully or sometimes survive without their main owners running them. Businesses become high risks when they have value to the extent that the owners are attending to them. If something happens to them, such as injury, illness or death, the value can immediately plummet.

Then there is ownership of collectibles such as art, antiques, classic cars or sports memorabilia. They all have value, but that value is only found if there is an able and willing buyer on the other side of the transaction. There are usually a limited number of interested buyers with the wherewithal to monetize the collection. This limitation on the number of possible buyers makes just about any category of collectible an illiquid asset.

Long-term annuities are another potential source of illiquidity. These are contracts with insurance companies that are one half insurance and one half investment. It's an agreement with an insurer that will provide an income stream for a stated period of time, sometimes a lifetime guarantee. In order to offer that kind of insurance, the companies lock your money up in long-term contracts that prevent you from getting your hands on it without assuming large losses or paying surrender charges.

If you find yourself suffering from illiquidity, the first thing to understand is that all is not lost with respect to this portion of your FlexScore. If everything goes well and you have assets that, albeit illiquid, still provide an income stream, then your ability to someday stop working and draw on income from these illiquid assets may very well remain intact. However, the risk exists that if your financial needs should change and you need to restructure these assets, their illiquidity ties your hands to a certain extent; you won't have much flexibility with your options of raising money. The best example of this danger is the so-called fire sale, where people basically liquidate possessions at a rapid pace with little regard for the prices they're receiving on their items. The sole objective of the fire sale is to raise as much cash as possible as quickly as possible. Buyers in these situations can score a windfall. Sellers can take a beating and end up committing a huge financial mistake out of simple desperation.

Say someone has worked an entire lifetime and is retiring soon to enjoy financial independence with a need for $5,000 a month of income to meet living expenses. Anyone who has worked to assemble a nest egg that will provide that much money is extremely fortunate. But if half of that income is derived from illiquid assets, the person will receive only half the available number of FlexScore points in this section. The risk is that half of the income is secure and half is not.

Illiquidity isn't the end of the world; however, it does increase the jeopardy of facing changing financial needs or economic reversals that could impact the quality and amount of your anticipated income stream.

If you're not on the verge of retirement and have some years remaining in your working life, you can evaluate how much of an income stream a liquid asset will supply contrasted with the same income revenue from an illiquid income stream. In today's economic environment the income stream you can expect from a liquid asset is not necessarily that high. So some people believe illiquid assets are better because they might provide more money. This may often be the case, but it does heighten one component of risk as you head towards financial independence.

If you're just now acquiring assets and funding your nest egg, as you make your investment decisions and aim for the highest returns possible make sure you don't forget to consider the risk illiquidity can present if one of the investments offers a high income stream even as it is illiquid. This factor may not govern your investment decision, but you should be aware of the potential for risk.

2. *You are not making investment decisions in keeping with your true risk tolerance (what we term asset diversification in Chapter Three).*

This means you are investing your money without matching your choice of investments with your tolerance for taking risks. Gauging your risk tolerance can be seen from two different perspectives.

You can say you are a five on a risk tolerance scale ranging from one to 10. This would define someone willing to take a moderate level of risk. But in reality you might have your investments tied up in conservative products such as CDs, short-term U.S. Treasury bonds and money market cash-style accounts. They all yield relatively low rates of return. They should be part of a diversified investment portfolio. But if they make up the bulk of your nest egg, you are not meeting the profile of someone who presents him- or herself as a moderate-risk investor.

On the other side of the scale there are plenty of people who invest in higher risk, more exotic investment strategies they believe will produce a higher rate of return than a more moderate, balanced portfolio. Unfortunately, too many of these investors can't stomach that kind of risk. They end up staying up worrying at night, making knee-jerk decisions when those investments react to even temporary downturns in the market and being vulnerable to the whipsaw effect we described earlier, which can stymie the ability to realize defined goals for the future.

Dalbar is one of the nation's leading financial service market research firms. For some years, Dalbar has conducted annual studies to find out if the investment decisions made by investors affect the performance of their investments. This report covers returns of the Standard & Poor's 500 stock index over the last 20, 10 and five-year time frames, the average investor's returns over those same time periods and the rate of inflation during these times.

Dalbar reveals that the average investor's return was typically much lower than the average investment return. Because investors fall victim to the emotion of the moment, they sometimes get out of investments at the wrong time. This process repeated time and again can cause the actual return an investor receives to be much different than the return achieved by the investments themselves. Doesn't seem to make sense, does it? Here's why it does: Between 1991 and 2011, the average stock investment as measured by the S&P 500 returned a 7.81 percent rate of return, but the average stock investor only saw about a 3.49 percent rate of return. The reason for this discrepancy lies within what our profession terms "behavioral finance." Investors don't necessarily follow a consistent strategy.

Here's how investment advisor Chad Griffeth described the problem:

> [P]eople have gone through the 'dot.com' and 'mortgage crisis' bubbles. People are learning to avoid some of the behaviors that result from the greed and fear we experienced during those periods. In reality though, we see these harmful behaviors more often than not when working with investors. If we simply remember that human nature can often tell us to do the wrong thing at the wrong time, we can help ourselves and our portfolios.

We know many investors who own concentrated blocks of stock. They put a lot of their money into very few investments. They feel comfortable with this investment strategy because they perceive the risks to be less than they are since they think they know everything there is to know about these investments. These people can be employees of publicly traded companies who own blocks of their own employers' stocks. They can have inherited the stock from relatives who earned quite a bit of money from these investments and they decide to hold onto them out of feelings of loyalty or obligation. The reasons don't matter. People justify to themselves why it makes sense for them to take on oversized amounts of risk.

Yet it is the amount of risk you assume that is paramount in ensuring a consistent rate of return on your investments because your personality and tolerance for risk will be with you for a long time. These things don't change greatly with the ebbs and flows of the economy. The amount of investment risk you can manage determines your long-term investment performance.

Say we promise to hand you the lump sum of $100,000. You are required to choose one of two different kinds of investments for these funds and keep the money invested there over a five-year period. At the end of that time you keep the interest and any gains you make on the $100,000, and then give the money back to us.

Now let's turn to the table below, which is very similar to what we showed you in Chapter Seven.

Year	Investment A (+) or (-)	Investment B (+) or (-)
1	+8%	+20%
2	+8%	+21%
3	+8%	+10%
4	+8%	-16%
5	+8%	+10%

(Source: Investment managers Atalanta Sosnoff and Eagle Asset Management.)

You can choose Investment A, where you will earn an 8 percent return over each of the five years. Or you can select Investment B, which as you can see is a lot more volatile. In either case you get to keep whatever returns you receive after five years.

Investment A looks very consistent, and very boring: Eight percent year after year each year for five years. Investment B boasts four years of double-digit returns, including one year of 20-plus percent. But it also includes one year with a negative return. Which investment strategy would you choose?

The answer is that it doesn't matter. In reality, you will have earned the exact same amount of money from both types of investment, an average of 8 percent per year, at the end of the five years. There is one difference: If, in looking into the future while you choose your investment type, you believe you will be bored and dissatisfied by seeing the same moderate return rate in each of the five years, you may take the greater risks and try to achieve a higher rate of return. You won't make any more money. But you will have to tolerate the volatility that comes with riskier investments that you think will generate higher return rates. The other reality is, if this example was in the real world, without restrictions on moving your money from one type of investment to another over five years, there is the very real danger that you will go off course, arbitrarily switch your investment strategy to a riskier portfolio and end up earning less than eight percent. In other words, you could easily get whipsawed.

The Dalbar studies regularly document this danger for investors and help make the point that a consistent rate of return is better than a volatile rate of return because human beings handle consistency much better than volatility.

What do you do if you've adopted the wrong investment strategy? First, you need to identify the correct investment strategy for you, given your appetite for risk. Then analyze your current investments to see if they are in alignment with that strategy. Once you understand your genuine tolerance for risk, then set a ceiling on the maximum amount of money you will put into more risky investments and don't exceed it. If your alignment of investments isn't correct, fix it.

Broadly speaking, if you find yourself in the middle of the road when it comes to taking investment risk, you want to have no more than 50 or 60 percent of your account value invested in risky assets, which means anything invested in the stock market. This is how the big pension, endowment and foundation funds invest their money. Once you adopt this practice, stick with it. When you don't stick with it and take more risks when you "feel good" because the markets are performing well and then panic when the markets experience downturns and sell off, it makes as much sense as driving down a wide open road and frequently alternating between 65 and 85 miles an hour. All you've done is take more risk and use more fuel without making more progress. It simply doesn't make sense.

Very few things should change your tolerance for risk. One could be if you find yourself coming into a great deal of money, more than you would ever need to meet your present or future needs. In that case you could raise your risk tolerance because you wouldn't be as worried about losing some of your assets. On the flip side, this newfound wealth could convince you to put your money into lower-risk investments since the greater volume of your assets means you wouldn't need to earn a higher rate of return. In this case your investment strategy would shift from growing your money to protecting it.

Other reasons to change investment strategies could be the loss of a job, the loss or gain of a loved one who contributes to your income or a significant change in your life goals.

FlexScore offers valuable tools to help you understand how much risk you should take on given your tolerance for it and ultimately helps you invest your money based on that level of risk.

3. *You have too much debt or the wrong kind of debt.*

Not all debt is bad debt, as we've said before. Student loans and home mortgages are examples of fruitful debt. Both can be seen as investments that either produce a higher income or ownership of an appreciative asset. That's why most financial planners and FlexScore view them favorably.

The Internal Revenue Service agrees with the fact that the assumption of these two types of debt contribute to improving society because the IRS gives you ways to deduct the interest you pay on this debt. That is also why these sorts of debt usually have relatively low rates of interest associated with them.

However, too much of a good thing can still be bad. The question is how much is too much? (As FlexScore measures how much debt you have, it is separated into housing debt versus consumer debt.)

Having too much housing debt is one way it can be bad. (It's what we called monthly housing cost ratio in Chapter Three.) One way to determine if you're spending too much on your housing is to draw on what most bank underwriting departments have used for decades, which is a ratio of how much you spend each month on housing costs (your mortgage and interest payments, property taxes, homeowner insurance and homeowner association fees) versus the amount of your monthly income. Underwriters generically call this your debt-to-income ratio. The figure they've established and applied for years is 28 percent. That means if you have a gross income of, let's say, $60,000 a year and your monthly income is $5,000, then you should consider keeping your total housing costs at no more than $1,400 a month, which would be 28 percent of your gross monthly income.

So examine your total mortgage costs plus insurance, property taxes and homeowner fees. If they add up to more than 28 percent of your gross monthly income, you've taken too big a housing bite. The obvious solution is to downsize. If it's not financially practical to make that move at this time, the next way to solve the problem is to increase your income. How do you go about doing that?

Is there anyone in the household contributing to the household expenses but not contributing to the household income, and realistically can? Find a way for them to get a part-time job to increase the family revenue so your gross monthly income rises high enough to make your overall housing costs more affordable.

The goal of staying below a 28 percent housing debt-to-income ratio is one that has been observed by banks for decades. That isn't to say if you have a 29 or 30 percent ratio you're going to go bankrupt within six months. However, every percentage of your income that is going somewhere else isn't going to build your financial future. And lowering your debt to income ratio will increase your FlexScore.

Having too much consumer debt is a different issue. (We describe it as consumer debt ratio in Chapter Three.) Some kinds of consumer debt such as student loans can be positive, as we've noted, but only in moderation. Student debt should be analyzed based on how much of a better lifetime income stream your education can supply.

For example, one of our clients in his mid-30s finished his final year of university studies when he was 31 years old with $500,000 in outstanding student loans. Before you think a typo was made, consider that his schooling was so expensive not only because he attended a prestigious private university but also because he earned both undergraduate and professional veterinary school degrees. Still, $500,000 in debt can put a lot of people underwater financially forever.

However, in his first year practicing as a veterinarian, our client was able to begin pulling down $300,000 a year. He was quickly well on his way to paying off his student debt. Now he is in his fifth year as a veterinarian, making more than $450,000 a year. He should pay off all of his remaining student loans within in the next 18 months. The point: Our client's numbers are indeed big, yet people should consider the same kind of equation when determining how much student debt they should accept. They should estimate how much they will earn after finishing their education. If you are going to compile $500,000 in debt after college, end up with a degree in English and teach high school students, that may not be such a good thing, strictly from a financial planning point of view.

An acquaintance graduated with a law degree from Georgetown University in Washington, D.C., one of the most prestigious law programs in the country, with nearly $100,000 in student loan debt. He is having a difficult time finding employment that will enable him to pay off the debt within a reasonable period of time because the field of law in which he specialized is so saturated. The point is to make sure you can get a job in your field of study in order to have the ability to pay back your debt.

Other than housing and student loan debt, there is nothing attractive or noble about carrying personal debt for any other reason. Personal debt includes credit cards, auto loans, home equity loans where you can write off interest payments (if you use the money from the loan improperly), personally secured loans from banks and any other private loans you can take on from any number or types of institutions or individuals.

What's wrong with these types of loans? They all amount to money you spent that you didn't have to begin with. If you didn't have the money to begin with, your assumption is you will have more money in the future with which to pay back the debts. Unfortunately, that doesn't always happen because, as described previously in this book, as more money comes in the front door we tend to spend more and more out the back door. We always seem to find a way to increase our lifestyle when our pay goes up. We usually find it impossible to adjust our lifestyle and spending downwards when our pay goes down.

A perfect robotic imitation of a human being would operate on the principle that every increase in income that comes in should first go back towards paying down existing debt. But we're not all robots and we're not all perfect financial beings. We tend to want to reward ourselves first and be disciplined second.

Of all the versions of bad debt, credit card debt is the most insidious. It has been too easy to obtain access to credit cards. Credit card corporations begin targeting you in college. You can get a $1,000 line of credit with a major credit card company as an 18 year old with no employment history and no credit rating whatsoever. Recent reforms imposed more regulation on the credit card industry and mitigated the abuse of credit cards by their suppliers, but it is still not that difficult to obtain credit cards.

Many large financial institutions that issue credit cards or personal loans use a formula similar to the one lenders employ to rule on qualifications for home mortgages. The longtime industry standard is that the totality of your monthly consumer debt payments should not exceed 20 percent of your gross monthly income. Using the same example as above, if someone earns $60,000 a year or $5,000 a month, no more than 20 percent of that income, or $1,000 a month, should be dedicated to paying off all forms of consumer debt, including student loans.

Let's look more closely at credit card debt. As we've already noted, nobody should be carrying month-to-month balances on their credit cards. With that said, it is an all-too-common problem that many Americans confront.

The key is realizing that the problem gets worse as soon as you start adding fuel to the fire. If you continue spending money with credit cards without paying off balances, you end up diverting scarce monthly income to paying off interest charges. This is money that could go for much more fruitful purposes such as preparing for your financial future.

The dilemma with debt has grown so commonplace that many people believe it's important to use your credit cards in order to maintain a good credit score. Let us say that again: People are fooled into thinking they won't have a good credit score if they don't use their credit cards. In truth, there are much better ways to maintain good credit than keeping high credit card balances.

Some think they should use their credit cards more often to earn bonus miles on airlines or points toward bonus programs that credit card companies promote to get you to keep using them. Those also aren't good enough reasons to incur more of this kind of negative debt that holds you hostage to high repayment rates.

When it comes to combating this epidemic the first step is denying the ability to dig yourself deeper into the debt hole. You do that by simply cutting up your credit cards so you will stop using them.

The second step is evaluating whether there are ways to reduce your debt by selling off the things you don't need, the things on which you are making payments. It could be that oversized and expensive car that you don't need when a more modest vehicle can deliver you from one place to another. It could be that boat you rarely use. Sometimes it has to be as dramatic as downsizing that too big and expensive house you own in exchange for a home with more reasonable mortgage payments.

Once you employ the first two steps, it's a matter of gradually paying off the debts you still owe. You realize the money that goes towards paying off debt cannot be used to build a nest egg that will eventually bring you financial freedom. But paying down debt will free up monthly interest charges that can go towards building for the future.

If you add the maximum percent of your monthly income going to paying for housing (28 percent) and paying down consumer debt (20 percent), this means nearly half, or 48 percent, of your gross income is going to paying back money you've already spent. This is why people can't look at debt as something they can take on today and figure out tomorrow. Debt is very sticky. If you can prevent yourself from paying $1 out of every $2 you earn every month on paying down debt, you will be well ahead of the game.

If you find yourself with a lot of debt, the trick is getting out of it or paying it off as soon as you can. That will free up more opportunities to spend your hard-earned money on more productive endeavors.

4. You haven't saved enough to fund your future financial independence. This amounts to what you've saved up until now (which is entitled "staying on pace to meet your goals" in Chapter Three).

This dilemma is not unlike what many students experience at some point in their high school or college years. They have a big class project due on Friday. It's Thursday afternoon before they have given any real thought to the assignment. Financial planners know, based on your goals and the most suitable rate of return you can realistically plan to achieve, how much you should have saved up for retirement at any given point in your financial life.

If you're behind, the most obvious way to fix the problem is increasing the amount you're putting into savings to close the gap between how much you have saved and how much you should have saved at this point given your goals. It's like running a 26.2-mile marathon. If you want to run it under four hours, the goal for most serious marathoners, you have to run on average a 9 minute 16 second mile. If you run the first 20 miles at an average of a 10 minute mile, the last six miles have to be run at a really fast pace. You have to run much harder the last six miles to make up for not having run fast enough during the first 20 miles.

If after hearing the starting gun kick off the marathon you lie down and take a nap, you're going to have some serious challenges making it through. The issue isn't the ability to run a 9 minute and 16 second mile. That's not hard for someone in good physical shape. The issue is running that 9 minute, 16 second mile consistently for each of the 26.2 miles.

When it comes to your financial affairs, if you get on pace and stay on pace by contributing a relatively small percentage of your monthly household income beginning in your younger earning years, you won't have to do as much in your later years when you've become accustomed to a certain lifestyle. This gets back to the importance of keeping debt low over the years.

For older people approaching retirement age, it will be very difficult to substantially make up for lost time. Again, the only practical solution may well be to readjust your goals.

5. You are not saving enough money for the future to meet your stated goal of financial independence. This covers how much you put away on a frequent basis from this point forward until you decide to stop working (also covered under "staying on pace to meet your goals" in Chapter Three).

This is closely related to not having saved enough up until this point (No. 4 above). It also probably results from the same flawed financial behaviors, which are all too typical in our nation. The most common question we get from the thousands of retirement plan participants we advise through their companies is, "Am I saving enough if I dedicate 'X' percent of my income or 'X' dollars per paycheck every month?"

Our answer is, we don't know. There is no rule of thumb. It's entirely dependent on how much one needs to support their lifestyle choices. Oftentimes, plan participants are shocked to learn how much they need to put away monthly to replace their current income at retirement age. That can flip people out. A 32-year old is shocked to know he or she has to be saving several hundred dollars a month to replace current income upon retirement. Most employees can't conceive of having to squirrel away that much money today for the future. But by waiting until later in life to begin, the journey to financial security becomes that much more difficult. You have less time for your money to grow and compound. There is less time to weather tough economic times and market downturns. You essentially give yourself zero wiggle room for error.

It's better to start young with a relatively modest level of contributions towards securing your future than having to put a much larger percentage of your income away later in life when you're already used to living on what you make and when so much of your paycheck is already earmarked for all the things you need to pay for. People adapt over time to what they live on. It's really hard for most people to take a "pay cut," which is how many view contributing to the company or their own retirement plan.

"That's crazy. I can't afford to save that much money every month," people tell themselves when facing the need to contribute into a retirement account. Actually, it's crazy that you can't afford not to do it if you ever want to achieve the financial independence many Americans strive to accomplish or claim they strive to accomplish.

Okay, what do you do if you haven't saved enough? You need to take a very close look at your monthly expenditures. That can mean a spreadsheet listing all of your expenses and categorizing where all the money is going. FlexScore has a tool you can use to do this. Most people's banks also let customers categorize their expenditures using online tools on the bank's website.

The initial step, as we've mentioned in previous chapters, is separating those expenditures into those involving your real needs (what you really need to spend to survive) and those that are wants, (things you can really do without if necessary). This may seem obvious or old-fashioned, but you'd be surprised at the number of people who have never gone through this exercise. You may discover some sizeable expenditures you think you need, but that you don't really require or that you could do without because they're not more important than providing for your financial future.

You will also more than likely discover that your needs side of the spreadsheet contains some items you can downsize to save money. For example, so many of us shop at large multi-department warehouse outlets such as Costco, Target and WalMart. These days you can shop under one big roof for many different needs such as groceries, clothing, household goods and furniture as well as all the discretionary fun items. If under your needs side of the spreadsheet you list expenditures at stores such as these you need to further divide your receipts between expenditures that are needs and wants. (When you patronize a traditional supermarket, there aren't as many non-essential items that you can be enticed to buy.)

This style of detective approach to your spending helps you see and have productive conversations with your spouse or loved ones about areas where you can perhaps cut a few expenses and free up some extra cash flow.

As we've said, when our clients ask us about the right amount of money to save, we have no magical response. The answer is different for every person. But in terms of how you prioritize saving in the monthly household budget, saving for your future should be about third, after housing and personal insurance needs. Personal finance industry experts point out that many people spend more on depreciating assets such as their cars (through monthly car loans or lease payments) than they save for their future. We've seen middle-aged couples with at least one teenage son or daughter that are making their own car payments and paying for the child's car. Each parent can have a monthly auto payment of roughly $500; the kid's car costs them another $250 a month. That's a total of $1,250 a month. Wrap your mind around whether this is okay. It is one thing if the same couple is putting away at least $1,250 a month in savings for their future. Or they may explain, "There's no way I can afford that kind of savings with the car payments we have now." Of the two options, which one do you think is more important: Making the car payments or contributing to your future? Which one will render greater long-range benefits?

The simple fact is that you should be saving more for retirement than you're spending on your vehicles. If you aren't, you should be.

Forty percent of Americans are saving nothing for retirement, according to the Federal Reserve, the U.S. Census Bureau and the Internal Revenue Service. Of those who are putting away something for the future, Americans on average are dedicating a little more than 2 percent of their income to savings.

A 2012 story broadcast on National Public Radio showed that the poor, middle class and wealthy all spend big percentages of their household budgets on shelter and more or less comparable proportions on fundamentals such as food and clothing. Yet the wealthy families target "a much, much bigger share [of their budgets] to saving for retirement." Saving for retirement took up 2.6 percent of budgets for households with incomes of $15,000 to

$19,999, 9.6 percent for households with incomes of $50,000 to $69,999, and 15.9 percent for households of $150,000 or above. Is it just because rich people have larger household budgets? Or do they know something other people don't?

There's no big secret here. Examine your expenditures. Get them down. Put the extra money into savings. It's really simple.

Someone hands you a bucket of water. It may be adequate to put out a campfire, but it won't help at all if a house is on fire. If there isn't time to accumulate enough resources to fund retirement at the age and income level you desire, then you need to reevaluate your goals.

CHAPTER NINE

Can I Retire Before Hitting 1,000?

*"Someone's sitting in the shade today because
someone else planted a tree a long time ago."*

—**Warren Buffett**, business magnate/investor and philanthropist

We've concentrated on the concept of retirement in this book. It's not a hard and fast age or date by which you will stop working. It is the confluence of two measures of preparation that come completely independent of each other: When you are mentally prepared to retire and when you are financially prepared to retire.

So retirement doesn't necessarily arrive at age 60 or 62 or 65 or 70. The more you think of retirement as gray hair and spending time with grandchildren, the more you will likely put off the hard work of preparing yourself for financial independence, which is what it takes to retire. When that day happens is primarily up to you as an individual.

FlexScore is simply an objective measurement of your financial preparedness. It measures how well you've done to date in preparing for your financial future as well as your trajectory from today forward. If your score is relatively low, let's say below 800 out of a maximum of 1,000 points, as you enter the so-called golden years, those years may not be so golden or they may not be so golden forever.

Imagine a squirrel whose main task in life is to store away enough nuts to carry it through the winter months. If the squirrel goofs around until seeing the leaves begin to turn during the fall months, it will likely be behind in preparing for the long and hard winter compared to its squirrel peers.

If you look at your time after work as a period of winter, unless you know for sure it will be a short winter (that you will die quickly after retiring) then exiting your income-earning years with a comparatively low FlexScore could be the biggest mistake you make in your life. The end result in a worst-case scenario is finding yourself running out of money before you run out of life. Then your subsistence consists of monthly benefits from the government in the form of Social Security or welfare or becoming a burden on your family members.

A popular 2006 Hollywood comedy called "Last Holiday" starring Queen Latifah tells the story of a working woman who is falsely diagnosed with a fatal illness and told she only has a matter of weeks to live. She cashes out her retirement savings and heads to a luxury resort in the Czech Republic, determined to spend every last cent of her money. At the end of the film, she learns she isn't going to die, hooks up with the man of her dreams and lives happily ever after. It's a great story, but one usually limited to Hollywood. The truth is that we usually don't control when we will die and can't predict it. So the smart option is to play the game of life well.

Running out of money before running out of life is the biggest fear described by typical clients with whom we work as they near the age of retirement; they don't want to rely on financial help from their children or loved ones. Accepting such help would require swallowing a certain amount of pride. To avoid it you need to face the fact that you haven't yet taken the necessary steps when you need to do so, which is while you are working.

Let's say you need to drive 90 miles to an important appointment scheduled for an hour from now. Getting there on time normally takes you an hour and a half driving at the speed limit with little or no traffic or congestion on the roadways. Can you make the trip in one hour's time? The answer technically is "yes" as long as several contingencies turn out in your favor and you enjoy no small amount of luck. First, you have to hit absolutely no traffic. Second, you need to be comfortable and adept at driving well above the speed limit, which most people are not. Third, you have to hope the enforcers of the law, the local highway patrol or state troopers, are out chasing other speeders going faster than you are. Let's say you do make it on time. Was that a safe or responsible way to travel? If you had experienced a blowout while driving at such a high rate of speed, what could have happened to your vehicle, let alone to your life?

If you have a relatively low FlexScore because you haven't made the proper financial preparations for retirement, can you still retire? Yes, but like our errant motorist who didn't leave far enough in advance to make the appointment, you go into retirement knowing the risks you take are much higher than other people who have properly prepared financially.

Warren Buffett once said, "Someone's sitting in the shade today because someone else planted a tree a long time ago." Another version of Buffett's sage observation comes from an anonymous source: "The best time to plant a tree is 20 years ago. The second best time is today."

If you are reading this and you are in your mid-20s, what a great opportunity you face. By doing just a little today you can guarantee financial freedom for yourself in the future.

If you're in your mid-30s and reading this but haven't started doing anything to prepare for your financial future, yesterday was the best day to start. Today is also a good day to begin. Tomorrow may be too late. This book, and FlexScore, should be a wake up call.

If you are in your mid-40s and haven't yet started to prepare we're not nearly as optimistic as if you were in your mid-30s. Still, with some diligence and discipline, financial independence can still be possible before you get older.

If you are in your mid-50s and haven't prepared, we don't have less hope, but we have news for you: Unless you are willing to work until your mid-70s, the likelihood of running out of money before you run out of life is much higher than the person who began preparing much earlier. At this age, you're no longer in the starting blocks; you've rounded the final curve and are entering the home stretch in the race of life.

A publishing company executive who was forced into retirement at an earlier age runs a blog offering advice for Baby Boomers (those born between 1946 and 1960) about health, finance and retirement. He raised the question about what you really need to have in retirement in order to live a satisfied life when he wrote, "If you retire early, you will probably have to watch your expenses and live a more modest lifestyle. You'll be poorer, but you might be happier."

"Be more with less" is a web site operated by Courtney Carver, who describes herself as an "aspiring minimalist." In a recent piece she posted entitled, "10 Ways You Can Have Enough Money and Stuff," she asks, "Do you have enough (too much)?" Spend a few moments taking to heart some of the points she makes:

- Count the number of clothes you have and divide that by 7. That is how many pieces of clothing you have to wear each day to use everything you have over the course of a week.
- Count how many utensils you own (forks, knives, spoons, whisks, peelers, all of them) and divide that by 7.
- Count how many apps, songs, games and videos you have on your computer and divide that by 7.
- Count how many TV channels, radio stations, CDs, DVDs, and games and divide that by 7.

It is very likely that you could live and thrive with less than 50 percent of what you own right now. And if you need less than half of the stuff, you probably need less than half of the space and less than half of the money it takes to maintain the stuff and the space. (Insert light bulb moment here!)

Carver poses additional questions you can answer about having a better life:

- If you had no debt, no monthly payments, what could you live on?
- If you didn't have to save for a nicer car, bigger house or extravagant vacation, what could you save for?
- What could you sell to pay off your debt?
- If you didn't have to dine out several times a week, how much could you give?
- If one is enough, what could you donate?

It's possible that you have been chasing more for so long that you forgot why you started the race in the first place. That is exactly what happened to me. If you can't answer, 'why,' you are on the wrong track. If your answer to 'why' is 'I don't know,' you are lost. You have to stop and start over.

We've asked before in this book about what else you could do with all that money from your monthly budget that goes to paying for that too big a car or house or all the expensive gadgets and toys you don't really need.

We're not saying that a minimalist lifestyle is the way to go. But asking and attempting to answer these questions is an instructive exercise at some point in everyone's life. They are especially relevant if you find yourself well behind the eight ball in preparing for your life after work.

The day you retire is the last day you have the ability to save for your retirement because you are no longer making an income from work. At that point, you are then living on the assets you built up during your working career. You have to measure the amount of happiness that might come from retiring early and financially unprepared against the potential stress that comes from a lack of financial flexibility. Financial stress can eat into your happiness more quickly than other factors. Some people can handle the stress; others can't nearly as well.

When flying in an aircraft over the ocean how do you know how far you can travel away from the land and above the water before having to turn back because you won't have enough fuel to make it to your destination? Headwinds and tailwinds can have a major impact on your calculations. You need to ensure there is enough fuel to traverse the ocean before you take off or else you must plan to put the plane down in the middle of the sea, hoping you crash safely and that someone will rescue you. Your investment portfolio has a big impact on your personal finances, just like having the right amount of fuel affects your ability to fly over the ocean. Applying these metaphors to financial affairs, you need to make sure your investment portfolio is large enough to withstand some normal headwinds and tailwinds so that you run out of life before you run out of money.

Let's discuss the options for those who haven't adequately prepared; that is they have a lower FlexScore and possess the mental desire to retire soon.

Jason's father vowed for years that he would retire as a manager at United Parcel Service, UPS, at the age of 55. When he turned 53, Jason's mother purchased one of those 24-month calendars. On the first month she wrote in big, bold numerals "24" in the middle of the month to signify how many more months he had to endure at work before retirement. He was mentally ready to retire at 55, to say the least. When his 55th birthday arrived, he retired. Thankfully, Jason's dad had prepared by saving enough money to quit working. But what if he hadn't? How could he have gotten out of bed and gone to work the next day? Mentally he prepared himself for a number of years to stop working. In addition to the stress of having to work against his will and the sense of failure, by age 55 he had already suffered three heart attacks and may not have had the ability to work any longer. The thought of working one more day never entered his mind.

What do you do if your mental preparedness gets ahead of your financial preparedness? Here are the options. They are listed in order, from the easiest to the hardest to accomplish; that also parallels the order in which people faced with this situation choose to adopt them.

Option One: If Jason's father had not prepared financially, he could have delayed retirement and continued working, which wasn't an option for him because mentally he was done with his career. We've had clients who were not financially ready to retire tell us in response to our news that retirement wasn't possible given their financial situation, "It doesn't matter; I'm done!"

Option Two: Find some kind of part-time job and keep one foot in (semi) retirement and the other foot in the world of work. You can move from working 40 hours a week to 15 or 20 hours. We've had clients who declare, "Oh, I'll just become a consultant," and end up doing the same kind of work in the same industry or occupation, whether for the past employer or for a new entity.

Option three: Austerity. It can be forced upon individuals as well as countries. Reduce your lifestyle. Reduce your monthly expenses to meet your lower level of income after retirement. (See our discussion on minimizing or downsizing your lifestyle above.) This is an option, but austerity hasn't been well received recently among many European nations and it isn't usually well accepted among individual households. In fact, we've never met or worked with clients who are willing to take major pay cuts; in other words adjust to the more limited lifestyle they can afford when they haven't prepared financially.

Of all the many clients we have counseled over the years who found themselves unprepared for retirement, not one person has made it through more than a full year by cutting down to the bone on his or her lifestyle. It just doesn't happen. People aren't prepared and don't believe they have to significantly adjust their expectations downward. We've even seen couples divorce over money issues in retirement because there wasn't enough of it.

What's the lesson? As early in life as possible set your mind on your financial ability to retire and not on your mental desire to do so.

Now let's take a look at some real life examples taken from among our own clients that illustrate each of the options we've touched upon.

Option One: *Keep working.* This might seem like an insurmountable obstacle to overcome for those who have a retirement date and age in mind. Change is something we all have to adjust to, albeit sometimes slowly or reluctantly. But take us at our word based upon our experience working with thousands of people: This is probably the easiest way to mitigate the risk of approaching the typical retirement age with a low FlexScore. What might this option entail? It depends on your current occupation and condition.

People in a more white-collar profession can ideally remain in the same place, doing the same work for the same income level. Those who are working in a very physically and mentally demanding job or field may want to consider finding a position at the same company or in the same industry that allows them to still enjoy the income stream to which they've become accustomed but without the day-to-day physical demands or mental strain.

You can't predict unforeseen circumstance such as a crippling injury or illness. We've had clients who weren't mentally or financially prepared for retirement but had to stop working, some with only a few years left to that planned retirement date, because of ailments such as a stroke, heart attack or Parkinson's disease.

One client, a man in his mid-60s, was a supervisor at a local manufacturing facility. He was mentally prepared for retirement, but also knew he needed to do a little more to be financially prepared. He was conservative and disciplined in his approach, which was admirable. We met twice a year for three years leading up to his retirement so he could be absolutely certain he was financially ready. During these final three years he made some minor spending adjustments at home in order to defer more money into his company 401(k) retirement plan.

He was finally ready. The big day arrived. He retired on July 30, and quickly took off on a celebratory weeklong hunting trip he had planned for years with his lifelong buddies. He passed away November 1, at the age of 66, from a previously undiagnosed disease some 90 days after achieving his long-sought goal of retiring. A sad story, but it can happen. The point is that we aren't simply pounding the table and telling everybody they need to work themselves to the edge of death right before retiring. We're only saying that none of us know when our last day will be. Even good intentions and excellent planning can be thwarted by the unexpected. But if you enter retirement fully knowing you are financially unprepared, don't expect much more than a hard time.

We could never have the patience to be schoolteachers, working all day, year after year with elementary, middle or high school students. It's a noble profession. Being a good teacher and really caring about the kids takes a lot of concentrated attention and energy. A common thought expressed by a lot of our clients who are nearing retirement as effective and conscientious teachers is, "There's no way I can work much longer with these kids and maintain the level of effectiveness they and their parents have a right to expect." You don't need to be a teacher who has spent a career working with students to know you have to constantly give it your all.

When Monday comes around and you don't look forward to

going back into the classroom, that's the time when you want to consider retiring. Public school teachers usually benefit from a decent defined-benefit pension plan. But perhaps teachers who find themselves with a low FlexScore and needing to work several more years in order to leave the work force don't have to focus so much on those needy kids or whatever part of their occupation causes them angst. One alternative is finding a way to work three or five more years. We've had teacher clients who adamantly insisted on retiring but somehow found a way to continue working in their profession by becoming resource specialists, counselors or consultants in their school districts. Some of them helped train new teachers. Anything that helped avoid the stress and still let them maintain the income was great.

So, no matter what your profession, the best first option is to consider how you can remain in your same industry, field or career and simply do something less taxing. Who knows? Maybe you'll discover a love for your new job and end up becoming energized in a way you couldn't predict.

Option Two: *Find part-time work.* This is when you're finished working as you have and can't do it any longer. Sometimes you're forced into this predicament because you lose your job or suffer an illness or injury. Don't count yourself out of the job market entirely. An old saying offers a way out: Where there's a will there's a way.

We know of many clients who are willing to work but are tired of doing it the same way they've been doing it. So they took on part time work doing something they always wanted to do but couldn't afford to either because the pay was too low or they didn't have the time while they were working their regular jobs. Some people find this "second career" even more fulfilling than their first career, giving them a new spring in their step and a new lease on life.

"Baby Boomers Search for Second Careers," read the headline in a June 2012 issue of U.S. News & World Report.

"Many baby boomers plan to keep working in some capacity after retirement," the story began. "While people will delay retirement because they need the money, others will take a job to ward off boredom and keep busy…Many baby boomers, who have already begun to reach age 65, are far from physically exhausted and often have much more to give." What's more, the article pointed out, "Delaying retirement doesn't have to mean continuing on a full-time job you hate. Senior citizens may feel they have had enough of their current career, after 30 or more years in the workforce. But many people still have the energy and drive to be active contributors to their community in a different capacity."

"A growing number of baby boomers are shunning retirement by pursuing late-life second careers that combine social goals and extra income," according to another piece in Inc. magazine in 2008.

We have some clients who took retail jobs at clothing outlets or arts and crafts stores, where they sold products they knew a lot about and enjoyed using. Some turned longtime hobbies into moneymaking endeavors. One client enjoyed classic cars, he became an auctioneer at classic car auctions held throughout California.

These sorts of jobs don't have to fulfill the same income quotient provided by the former full-time career. If they can supply an income of $1,000 a month or more that may be enough for you to end your regular employment and still be able to survive while enjoying a comfortable lifestyle. This supplemental income also allows you to avoid drawing at a higher rate on your nest egg, therefore permitting you to extend the amount of time you can be financially independent for as long as you can. Since your lifespan probably won't change, it also means you have fewer years upon which to draw down the nest egg, meaning your risk of running out of money before you run out of life is avoided or at least significantly reduced. So long as you maintain your health, this is an option worth considering.

Option Three: *Austerity.* It was defined a few years ago in the New Statesman, the British weekly current affairs magazine, as "a policy of deficit cutting by lowering spending via a reduction in the amount of benefits and public services provided." We have followed news coverage about the governments of southern European countries that have been compelled to accept major cutbacks in public benefits, services and payrolls causing lower standards of living and widespread unemployment. If austerity can be imposed on large entities such as national governments, it can also apply to individual households in the United States.

In theory, austerity simply means cutting back or eliminating those expenses that are not absolutely necessary for the survival of the household. One can theoretically take pen and paper plus a few ounces of logic, and try to eliminate expenditures they feel are superfluous. Unfortunately, there are dozens of cases where we have had to advise our clients that austerity is their only alternative. We haven't seen this option successfully adopted for more than a year's time. Some people initially accept the necessity of austerity, but have a hard time following through with it. Personal habits are set over time, often over a long period of time, and they are hard to change, especially later in life.

The analogy of dieting is instructive. People vow they will lose 30 pounds. They know they need to lose the weight and may stick to the diet for a while; they may even succeed in dropping some pounds. But sticking with it over time, taking off and keeping off the pounds, is much more challenging. The same goes with adopting and sticking with an austere household budget, even though it can solve the serious financial problems many people confront.

Of the three options available to people who haven't properly prepared financially, austerity is the least likely to be selected and the least likely to be adequately implemented.

The best answer for most people approaching the time they would like to retire with a low FlexScore is some combination of all three strategies. If we said to you, "Instead of having to work another 10 years at your current job, you could work five more years, your spouse could take on 15- to 20-hours a week of work and you could take a good sharp knife to your monthly expenses, searching for those where you are cutting fat but not meat so you don't have to live on a bare bones budget when the final day of work passes." Would those be more acceptable alternatives?

The important thing to remember with this and all financial advice is that the earlier you detect a problem and start seriously addressing it, the more options you will have.

CHAPTER TEN

How FlexScore Helps You Avoid Common Financial Failures

"Whether you think you can or you think you can't, you're right."

—Henry Ford

The average person spends less time every year planning for future financial independence than planning this year's vacation. Why? One aspect of planning is the more you look forward to something the more you want to plan for it. People look forward to their vacations so they spend more time planning them.

Achieving financial independence, being able to continue your current lifestyle without having to work, is like experiencing a permanent vacation. So you would think there would be plenty of motivation to plan for it. Yet neglecting to plan for the future is the most common financial failure. This chapter relates this and other failures and shows how FlexScore can help you avoid them.

A big financial impediment many people must learn to overcome is the law of large sums. You roll out of bed on your 40th birthday. You're 5'11" tall and weigh 285 pounds. All the standard medical charts along with your doctor say your weight should be about 185 pounds. But the idea of losing more than 100 pounds is so daunting that you have no idea of where to begin. But you do begin. You read a few articles, talk to some friends. Maybe your physician hands you a meal plan or sets you up with a dietician. You try your best to follow the diet and you start exercising.

You have a little success at the beginning. You lose some pounds. You start to feel better. After a while you start to plateau, which is natural. Then your bad habits start creeping back into your life. You eat that favorite food. You skip exercise sessions. At first you backslide only once a week, then twice a week. The weight comes back on and you give up because contemplating the burden of losing 100 pounds is just too great.

A few months go by and you decide to start again. You diet. You exercise. You lose weight. You stop dieting and exercising, and gain it all back again. The cycle keeps repeating itself. It's a series of fits and starts, all leading over time to very little progress.

The same phenomenon can be observed in saving up for your financial future. Many clients come in to see us. We offer advice and help them set their goals and devise a plan that will take them down the path towards financial freedom. They get motivated. A few months go by. They save a couple of bucks, according to the plan they've established. But then the time comes to plan the yearly family trip, and they can't resist the urge to upgrade the vacation. Or they want to improve upon the vehicle they're driving. Or buy that nice gadget they've been coveting. These opportunities arise when they see a little extra money in their account from the savings plan we helped them set up. They completely forget that the entire purpose of that cash is to provide for their future financial independence. So the money gets spent on something else and they're back at square one.

A few more months go by. Our clients realize they are still living paycheck to paycheck and remember why they don't like it. They think, "We gotta' do something different and better for ourselves." Just like the erratic dieter, they again begin the process of saving. They save. They feel good. They forget what the extra money is for. Something comes up. They money gets spent once more.

We don't usually work with people who are aspiring to have money. We work with people who have money. But we have a lot of friends and acquaintances who just can't seem to get their financial legs under them and put themselves in a better situation for the future. Many of these friends and acquaintances have the ability and the resources; the ingredient they're missing is the right attitude. We can usually tell during our first meetings with new clients which ones have the attitude to make it and which ones don't. It has nothing to do with how much money they are making or their educational or professional status. What counts are their attitude and ability to execute on the stated goals they have adopted, the ability to seriously tackle and actually complete their financial to-do list laid out by FlexScore.

Scripture teaches us to "act as if you have faith and faith will be given to you." Countless motivational speakers have more crudely adapted the Biblical lesson when they say, "Fake it until you make it." That means if you wake up every day with the attitude that you're going to become a success no matter what or that you're going to have a great day and triumph in your endeavors, it is very likely that you will succeed. Then your entire mindset is one that permits you to more easily take on life's challenges and travails, and dispatch them like water off the back of a duck.

Financial planning is no different. If you fake it until you make it and think of yourself as being responsible, as being a saver, then the behaviors that come along with that mindset will become much easier to adopt because you will embrace them as your own instead of thinking you have to become some other person you aren't. Constantly trying to convince yourself that you need to become like those "other people over there" is a monumental task. The chances are you will never become them.

When Jason was hired at the age of 26 by the prestigious former Solomon Smith Barney Wall Street brokerage firm, the branch manager told him at the very first official sales meeting, "You're out in the community, say at a cocktail party.

You're at one end of the room. Your wife is at the other. Things aren't going so well with your business. You know that. Your wife does too. But you can't tell anyone. When the person at the other end of the room asks your wife, 'So how are things going for your husband?' she can't hesitate or blink; she just says, 'Things are going wonderful. He's doing such a good job and he's really helped a lot of clients.' Because if she or you tell people it's not going well, then they all start talking about how it's not going well and the focus gets turned on all the negative energy. Versus saying things are going well because they need to be going well in your mind if everything is going to work out for you. If you're always negative or pessimistic or downtrodden or focused on what didn't happen, it's amazing how that thought of failure breeds more failure. It's a self-fulfilling prophecy.

The inverse is also true. Thoughts of success breed success. It's the power of thought. If you believe you'll be successful or if you believe you're going to fail, you will be correct in either case. It's that old line from Henry Ford: "Whether you think you can or you think you can't, you're right."

Now let's apply that principle to the law of large sums. When we sit down in a formal way with clients who need to understand how much they should be saving, we customarily start them off at the end result. After all, we say, all the work you do in your working years is a means to an end. The end result is to accumulate a large enough nest egg to support yourself all the way through the rest of your life after work. For most people earning about $50,000 a year who want to retire at age 62, the typical age at which most Americans say they want to retire, they need to have built up a nest egg of roughly $750,000 in savings, retirement accounts or investments plus Social Security benefits for both a husband and a wife. Yes, like you, we hope Social Security will be there, but you might not want to rely upon it too much, especially if you are less than 40 years of age.

Once that seemingly huge figure of $750,000 is staring people in the face, they have a choice. They can try to comprehend the real need they have to acquire that amount of money to meet their stated goals and work with us to create bite-sized action steps to get them there. Or they can remain in shock over that big sum and be paralyzed by the tasks ahead. If they make the latter choice, they will continue marching towards the inevitable with little or no preparation.

There is a scene in so many cartoons and motion pictures where people are on a raft floating down a river. The river picks up velocity and becomes a little more swift. The people on the raft adjust to the speed, remain on the raft and believe they're going to make it through. Around the bend they come; the river seems to calm itself and the rafters think they're going to be fine. But it's the calm before the storm. The calm water only signals that the river is widening because they're about to go over the edge of the massive waterfall.

That drill is what people too frequently do to themselves when it comes to preparing financially by saving and investing. They get by and do the bare minimum. They adjust to that inadequate measure. "Oh, they said I should start by saving 3 percent of my monthly income and I've been constantly doing that…for decades." But the changes they needed to make, such as boosting the percent of their income going into savings, were also constant. They can't just tell themselves, "I made that decision 30 years before my retirement and it will be the right direction to take me all the way through my working career." You need to set realistic goals and then objectively review where you're at in meeting those goals periodically, readjusting course when necessary.

Like the rafters, once you are accustomed to bumps in the water, you become a little complacent. You have to remind yourself that the water will at some point flow off the edge of the waterfall. So you can't just sit in the raft and adjust to momentary changes in conditions without planning for a way to get off the raft and out of the water to safety before the raft hits the waterfall. That's the secret. Your decision not to make a decision to get yourself prepared is a decision nonetheless. When it comes to your personal finances it is probably the worst decision you'll ever make.

You can always come up with a reason not to save or invest. You can always justify why you can't do it at any given moment.

People don't realize they need such a sum as $750,000 to become financially secure in retirement. You tell someone they need to have $750,000, which is 15 times their annual compensation, and they are incredulous. This is especially so when you're talking with 40 year olds who haven't started saving anything. They don't believe it because it sounds so crazy.

If building what seems to be such a formidable nest egg doesn't blow their minds, people completely deny the need to do it. "Oh, it won't take that much money to retire," they will say. "We don't live that luxurious a life."

"We're just trying to show you how much you need to continue the lifestyle you're leading now," we reply. Once people accept that reality the burden of building up such a big pot of money to replace today's income can appear overwhelming; they can get discouraged by the large numbers and shut down their efforts to achieve what is actually a very achievable goal.

One way to consider taking on a task that seems monumental is equating it to eating an elephant. How do you eat such a huge creature? The answer is one bite at a time. If you look at the elephant and think, "I gotta eat that?" the effort seems overwhelming. However, if you don't dwell on it that way and instead divide the large task into many small achievable steps, the entire elephant can be consumed. In the same manner, success can be had in achieving financial independence by planning to put away a little money at a time, time after time.

"People understand the complicated things pretty easily," farm labor and civil rights leader Cesar Chavez said. "It's the easy things most people have a hard time understanding." Community or union organizing, he added, is about "organizing one person at a time, time after time after time." It's a universal principle.

Now, let's take the case of one of our clients who started out in a blue-collar job at a manufacturing plant and worked his way up into a management position. He accumulated a good deal of tenure at his company where he did very well and was able to save up $750,000 in a 401(k) profit-sharing plan into which the firm put away most of the money for him. Upon retirement, he withdrew $75,000 a year to live on against our advice to withdraw a smaller annual sum. In any year in which you take out that amount of money from your portfolio but don't earn 10 percent growth, you begin eating into the principal amount needed to earn future interest to fund your retirement. At the time he retired, our guy experienced about three years in a row of very low returns on the stock market. The next thing he knew, between the low returns and withdrawing $75,000 a year, his $750,000 nest egg had shrunk to below $600,000. He forgot the second half of the equation: Even if you have the ability to save enough to retire, you can only afford to live on an amount withdrawn from your savings so that the portfolio will continue sustaining you for the rest of your life.

So the law of large sums has two sides: You need to get up that great big hill by acquiring the pot of money to fund your nest egg. Once on top of the hill, you can't come sliding all the way down well before your lifespan is up because you need that money to hopefully last a long time. Just because you deem yourself successful for having saved money, your job is not done. You now have to take care of that nest egg and make spending decisions based on preserving it on into the future. That large sum is meant to stay large so it can sustain you for the rest of your life. If you make poor decisions and start eating into the principal, you backtrack and end up being little better off than people who didn't save nearly as well as you did by the time they retired.

FlexScore helps you avoid this and other common pitfalls by keeping you focused. It supplies concepts, ideas, methodologies and realistic action steps to help you stay on track. Because it gives you a score, it encourages constant awareness of your status and allows you to closely monitor your progress towards your stated goals. It makes you think twice about making bad financial decisions because you can use this tool to immediately know the impacts those decisions will have on your score.

Another all too common mistake people make in their financial lives is letting their emotions get in the way of logic.

The financial news media is now ubiquitous; it can be found everywhere you look, especially on-line. It provides a service that some people confuse as advice. The service is offering information about updates on publicly traded companies, politicians' legislation and regulations having to do with financial matters, and trends in the overall economy. What it doesn't talk about is what you should do in your particular situation, because the media cannot comment on an individual's needs since it broadcasts information pertaining to all people's needs. That doesn't stop people who go to journalism school and write and report on financial matters from crossing the line from pure reporting to commenting on what people should do with their money. That's understandable. After all, the journalists' goal is to get people to read or view their work product in order to boost their readership or ratings. Unfortunately, one of the best ways to do that is to be loud and boisterous over financial issues. Turn the pages of the Wall Street Journal and you will find all sorts of information about the economy and publicly traded businesses. Or read Time magazine or watch the business news on cable networks or on network affiliate television stations. There is constant economic and financial talk, too frequently supplying information that is neither sound nor logical. All this media noise causes too many casual observers to respond emotionally to what is being written or discussed and to let those emotions control their decision-making.

In the American system of balanced and objective journalism what you're supposed to be reading in the straight news columns of the newspaper or seeing on news programs carried by the mainstream TV networks and affiliates is fair and balanced reporting. That means journalists present both or multiple sides of a story so everyone's opinion is represented. In other words, the reporter doesn't take sides, thereby allowing the readers or viewers to form their own opinions based on objective information. This is fundamentally different than editorials or opinion pieces in the op-ed pages of the newspaper where publishers or commentators are supposed to present their points of view.

That's how it is supposed to work. But that's not always the case in the real world.

When we were both with the big Wall Street firm Smith Barney there were professional economists in the firm whose job was to get onto the financial news channels to represent the company and express its varying points of view. For example, Tobias Levkovich always presented a doom and gloom view of financial markets and the economy. He would usually predict that the economy was going to fall and stall. John Manley was Levkovich's counterpart; he always predicted the economy and markets would be all wine and roses, and that they would go up and people didn't have to worry about extended bad markets. Each economist was regularly featured on CNN, CNBC, PBS and Wall Street Week. They were consistently quoted in the New York Times, Wall Street Journal, Chicago Tribune, Newsweek, USA Today, Barons, Business Week and Time.

We once had the opportunity to have dinner with John Manley

and asked him how he was able to appear so often on television shows and in all the major daily newspapers. "It's simple," he replied. "The news shows would call a number of people like myself and ask for our opinions. Their producers would search for the people who are the furthest apart in their perspectives, representing the most divergent views. That is who they would put on the show that day."

A high level executive with a major Wall Street brokerage firm told our training class at Solomon Smith Barney how one morning she woke up so sick in bed that she couldn't come to work. But she wanted to get caught up on the start of the financial markets that day. So she turned on her TV to catch the financial news at 9:30 a.m., just as the New York Stock Exchange was about to open. There was a veteran financial news reporter broadcasting live from the floor of the New York Stock Exchange. He was acting like a cheerleader, saying very excitedly, "The equity markets are about to open. There is so much news and data out today. It will be an exciting day on Wall Street. The opening bell is moments away." Then the bell rang and he got even more excited and energized.

This senior executive who could barely get out of bed because she was so sick found herself captivated and wound up by the news coverage she was viewing. Then she stopped and said to herself, "Wait a minute. This is just a news show. The markets open every day at 9:30 a.m. with the ringing of the same bell. This is nothing new or different. I'm falling victim to the same hype and excitement I always warn our firm's investors to guard against."

If a high level executive who knows better was duped, even momentarily, imagine how the average viewer can find him- or herself totally wrapped up in the emotion of the moment watching this financial programming. Remember, these are just television shows. Their purpose is to boost ratings by attracting and holding audiences. They do that by providing entertainment, some news and a good dose of controversy. All that does is create a lot of noise, but little insight, for the average investor. That noise can be counterproductive to people making objective, rational decisions about their personal finances. Investors can become paralyzed by the noise.

FlexScore helps you avoid this dilemma by offering a concrete score of your own financial preparedness based on time-tested standards and objective data. It does not fall prey to hype or the trend or flavor of the day on Wall Street or how the news media reports about Wall Street.

The amount of knowledge it takes to succeed financially doesn't require a Ph.D degree in finance or economics. It certainly requires more information than what people are typically taught in school or by their parents. Because of this knowledge gap, unwary people too easily glom onto get-rich-quick investment schemes or the latest fad on the best way to retire early. FlexScore is not magical. It does take that big elephant that seems so challenging to eat and breaks it down into one-piece-at-a-time solutions. FlexScore gives you little bits of real knowledge, not in the style of an academic dissertation, but in fun and easy appetizer bites.

When we hear people explain why they didn't start financial planning earlier in their lives, the most common conundrum is they didn't know where to start. The map to financial independence was so large that they didn't know how to draw a route to their destination. They often go on to relate how they considered meeting with a financial planner but didn't want him or her to be talking over their heads the entire time. So people find themselves not only lacking in knowledge but also lacking the motivation to get the knowledge because they think it is so high and far away from their ability to understand that the entire exercise will be futile.

How often are you or someone you know dissuaded from purchasing an item that requires assembly or comes with an instruction booklet so detailed that you think it takes an engineering degree to comprehend. Many people view financial affairs in much the same way. They know the subject can be arcane and complicated, and would rather put off the task of tackling the issue out of fear they won't be able to figure it out.

FlexScore delivers the bite-sized steps needed to succeed, one step at a time, time after time, and all in plain English. No prerequisite course or experience is needed to understand how FlexScore works before you can use it yourself. It works just as well for someone who is brand new to financial planning as it does for a person with decades of financial dealings under the belt. Most people's financial education comes from growing up with parents or family or from friends or co-workers. As we pointed out in this book, that education is usually woefully inadequate. Successfully navigating FlexScore doesn't require a degree in financial planning, although through its use you will feel like you earned one anyway, bolstered by the confidence your growing score can give you.

FlexScore also inoculates you against the latest get-rich-quick schemes, swindles and fancy fads or trends that can put your financial future at risk. People often opt for the easy way out if they believe so much financial knowledge is necessary to succeed or if they don't want to put the time or effort into gaining that knowledge. Personal testimonials about these scams and schemes abound. They are as common as the array of late-night infomercials boasting how easy it is to get rich by flipping houses or trading in the stock market using technical indicators or any number of multi-level marketing techniques. Do you ever notice the small type at the bottom of these paid programs where it says, "These results are not typical" or "Your results may vary"? Not everyone watching these shows see the disclaimers and those who do may choose to overlook them in the hope they will turn out just like the people on the television screen. Despite the warnings, the gullible people who buy into these shams don't see themselves as typical; they view themselves as special. The entire industry of get-rich-quick schemes ironically preys on the assumption that people will bypass the fundamentals of real financial planning and choose their easy alternatives. It's the same theory as the purveyors of fad diets; they tell people they can lose weight without dieting, exercising or exhibiting any discipline at all. None of these schemes work in the end, whether they are dietary or financial.

Overspending is at once the simplest and most difficult financial failure to overcome. The temptations constantly present themselves: More house. More car. More vacation. More everything. Falling victim to these temptations is made all the easier by the access to and technology of credit cards.

You access your bank account on-line. Before it even lets you into the system you have to maneuver through two boxes: Would you like to apply for more credit on your home or would you like to get the financial institution's new zero percent interest credit card? Since they already have all your financial information, there is no need to spend time filling out lengthy forms or answering questions. Just click here and you get the additional credit instantaneously. It's just like when you visit McDonald's and they ask whether you want to supersize your order. All you have to do is say, "Yes." It's easier than that with on-line banking because you can do it from the comfort of your own home with the simple click of a button on your computer.

We're not necessarily talking about the people who regularly waste their money buying frivolous gadgets or toys. These aren't your neighbors with the all-terrain vehicle or motor home, the nice boat and every room fitted with a giant-sized TV screen and the best surround sound system. It isn't the children next door with the most expensive designer clothes and the latest tech gadgets. It's not them. We already know they're irresponsible about how they misspend their money.

We're talking about the average American, maybe even you. When you're booking the family vacation to San Diego, do you allow the travel agent to stretch your budget from the moderate hotel and instead sell you on all the attractive benefits, bells and whistles of the five-star accommodations? It will only cost an extra $1,000, they say. Aren't you worth it? Or you go to buy the new car you need and let the sales person talk you out of the base model and into the fully loaded version of the same vehicle. It's only a little extra and it gets spread out over five years of payments anyway. Just because you're pre-approved for a certain mortgage amount, do you let the real estate agent convince you to get a bigger or better home by spending right up against the maximum limit? It doesn't seem to add that much to the monthly payment and after all it's amortized over 20 or 30 years.

We both had the same first time experience buying real estate some years ago. We told our real estate agents we wanted to look at $125,000 homes. With steady incomes and good credit, we were pre-approved for mortgages of up to $150,000. We made the mistake of showing our agents our pre-approval letters from the bank. What did the agents show us? Homes priced in the range of $150,000 to $160,000, because they saw we were pre-approved.

How many times have people advised you to always buy a little more home than you think you need? It's hard to ignore the advice. I'm approved for more money. I'm told I should do it. All of a sudden the decision to buy the bigger, more expensive home becomes so easy.

Everyone loves to own a new car. If you ask yourself why, you may start regurgitating what your friends tell you: You need a new car because of the warranty protection. It's safer. It has better fuel efficiency. But don't you need a car just to get from one place to another? And if it has air conditioning during the hot summer months, then it is all the better. If it was manufactured in the last decade it's likely going to be as safe, as fuel-efficient and as mechanically sound as a new model. So what you're really paying for in a new car is the new car smell. Is it worth paying the extra thousands of dollars for the smell that goes away quickly enough? When it comes to buying homes and cars don't just worry about your needs and wants; worry about your ability. Finance departments at auto dealerships and local mortgage lenders will not ask how much of a car or home you're looking to purchase. Their assumption is that by purchasing a vehicle or a house you will maximize your ability to finance it. Worry about this more: Maxing out your financial ability to make those purchases means you won't be left with much financial wiggle room to fund other pressing financial needs, such as saving for your future.

Ask yourself: Do you want to be the person with all the toys and extravagant spending habits? Do you want to be the person who bit off too big a chunk of house or car? Or do you want to be among the minority of practical people who don't supersize their lives and therefore have a better shot at a higher FlexScore? Depending on how you answer those questions, there may still be room for hope. Change is always possible, if there is the will.

This brings us to the principle that stuff is not as good as money and to the distinction between appreciating assets (that gain value with time) and depreciating assets (that lose value over time).

Having money matters, not having stuff. Surrounding yourself with the accoutrements of financial success, no matter how great or small, is a sure fire way to dilute your ability to actually achieve financial independence. The trappings of success have been discussed before in this book, but they are different for everybody.

A successful, high-income producing professional woman in her late 40s may stereotypically go out and buy that brand new convertible sports car as a trophy to show those around her that she has achieved something with her life. But no matter what she's trying to show others, the truth is what she achieved is nothing more than turning the opportunity to buy assets that appreciate in value into a purchase that will surely depreciate in value. Those who make decisions time and time again to surround themselves with the evidence of their so-called financial success will rarely truly achieve financial success. The resources they could use to build a large degree of financial security are wasted on goods or experiences that offer only momentary pleasure or satisfaction.

"Are you constipated with stuff?" asks Jessica Chapman, a professional organizer whose Sacramento-based consulting firm, Room to Breathe, helps people turn their homes and businesses into more clutter free and efficient environments. She asks her clients to think of their lives as if they were their bodies' digestive tracks: Are they running smoothly and flowing through or do people find themselves "a little constipated with stuff"? (Remember our mention of Courtney Carver, the aspiring minimalist who asks if we can "be more with less" in Chapter Nine?) The self-storage industry has been thriving for decades on the American ideal of super consumerism. People literally pay hundreds of dollars a month to store things they don't need and probably forgot about long ago.

The more you commit your resources, the chief among them being your income, towards buying stuff that won't help you meet your financial goals the longer your FlexScore will stagnate and fail to grow. FlexScore demonstrates the direct effect of taking discretionary income and using it to purchase appreciative assets you need that increase in value rather than buying depreciative assets that you probably don't need and that decrease in value. FlexScore helps you accurately predict your success when deciding to put cash into investments and other appreciative assets instead of wasting money on doing little more than trying to keep up with the Joneses. Your FlexScore will go up much more quickly by doing the former. If you can replace whatever fleeting pleasure you get from buying those superfluous goods or possessions with the feeling of genuine, long-lasting satisfaction that comes from watching your FlexScore rise you will be well on your way to financial independence.

"I'll start saving as soon as I make more money." Do you know how routinely we hear that excuse? The lady we meet at the gym comes in for financial advice. "I have to get out of debt before I can start saving," she avows. Reducing debt can be a good place to start. But being financially prepared is first and foremost about a mentality, not tactics. People will always come up with a reason why they can't do something. We all do it. Today the gym lady can't save because of the need to rid herself of debt. Tomorrow she's getting married. The next day it's the need to buy a car or a house or to help the kids through college. Soon the 22-year old fitness instructor is 42; she hasn't saved a damned thing because there's always the next financial obstacle to overcome first.

Procrastination based on excuses just impedes the future ability to control your finances. Putting off what you need to do today until tomorrow is a mistake. There's always a good reason to spend money on something else. When you make more you spend more. Human nature is not to save. Human nature is, "I have more money and now I can get that better car or that nicer house or take that better vacation or buy nicer clothes or eat at nicer restaurants." People piss money away, much more than they even realize.

No one does it quite the same way as other people they know. A lot of people look down on what others are doing with their money. They can be very judgmental. Yet those who are judging are frequently plagued by their own peculiar spending habits. Let's rattle off some for-instances, taken from among the clients we've served.

- ✓ A special set of golf clubs and the latest golf paraphernalia.
- ✓ Playing at more exclusive, and expensive, golf courses.
- ✓ Joining a more trendy fitness club and justifying it by the need to get in shape, even though it costs more than $100 a month.

- ✓ All that expensive new gym apparel.
- ✓ Going out more often to nicer restaurants.
- ✓ Cooking at home with all the latest kitchen gadgets and accompaniments.
- ✓ That wine tasting trip to those beautiful Napa Valley vintners where you join several wine-of-the-month clubs.
- ✓ The new upgraded guitar or musical instrument.
- ✓ Switching shopping from Target or Kohl's to Macy's or Nordstrom's.
- ✓ The newest style of seasonal women's shoes.
- ✓ The latest version of Kindle or other e-readers, replacing last year's model.
- ✓ The new fishing rod and reel.
- ✓ The latest toys for the kids they see advertised on TV.
- ✓ The radio-controlled toy plane.
- ✓ Real planes and flying lessons.
- ✓ Bicycling and all the things you can get that go with it.
- ✓ Car racing, as a spectator or participant.
- ✓ Trips to destination ski resorts.
- ✓ Hot air ballooning.
- ✓ Gambling, whether in Las Vegas or at "Indian" casinos.
- ✓ Woodworking.
- ✓ Pets, their care and comfort.
- ✓ Taking that extra monthly trip to the spa.
- ✓ The recent fad of ballroom dancing lessons.
- ✓ Memorabilia and collecting, from sports and political to cars and movies.
- ✓ Compiling and tracking fulfillment of your "bucket list."
- ✓ Seasonal tickets to sporting events, the theater or the symphony, and insisting on seats close to the action or the stage no matter what the costs (Jason wastes his money on this).
- ✓ The newest iPhone or Apple computer product (Jeff's choice).

Jason thinks Jeff's addiction to the latest high-tech gadget is a big waste of money because he assumes you can get just as much done with the last generation of technology. Jeff thinks Jason's addiction to front-row seats is a waste because you can hear the song just as well in the 12th row as in the 1st. Both of us justify our spending as helping us in other ways, but the common denominator is that we're both human and both of us spend money needlessly sometimes.

Are all of the things we listed frivolous? Not necessarily. Do all of them siphon off scarce resources that could go into building your financial future? Yes.

This is not to say people should deny themselves their passions or preferences. They just need to address them judiciously. Don't fool yourself into thinking that what you're doing is always fruitful and not a waste of money.

FlexScore helps you keep your hobbies and spending habits in check by constantly placing in front of you the real costs of maintaining these practices and, more importantly, by contrasting how much more mileage you can get from spending that money on building for your future.

"Time is on my side." We hear that said a lot too. "I can put off until tomorrow what I should do today because I still have plenty of time before I have to worry about becoming financially independent." Somehow, people in their 20s and 30s decide they don't need to take those tough steps towards financial security because they think they are so young, because financial planning is such an "old-person" thing to do and because the future seems so far away.

There's something about arriving at middle age that gives people a greater sense of immediacy when it comes to their financial preparedness. If that same sense of immediacy could be acquired 10, 15 or 20 years earlier, imagine how much closer and quicker you would be to reaching your financial goals. Then there is always the unforeseen or the unpredictable that can happen to you or a loved one, including illness, death, disability, unemployment or divorce, to name a few.

What if you had the power to glimpse into the future, something that is only possible in science fiction novels or films? With FlexScore, the financial trajectory you're on now can be observed far into the future. You can witness the real-life consequences of actions or inactions you take today. It allows you to have at your disposal one extra motivational tool other than that financially responsible friend or relative nagging you about how you're not doing the right thing.

Let's draw once more on the analogy of not eating right or exercising. What if your doctor could use a computer to draw a picture of what you will look like in 20 or 25 years and describe the consequences based on the current trajectory of your present eating and exercise habits? What if you could see for yourself the health effects your condition will produce well into the future? Might it convince you to change your habits?

On the other hand, if you could see the financial benefits of today's hard work and good decision-making projected into the future, would that increase the likelihood you would stick to the financial fundamentals and strive to adhere to the plan you have set for yourself? FlexScore does that for you.

"Debt is no big deal." Whether they believe it or not, people say that to themselves every time they make a purchase on credit, buy too big a car or house or make some other unwise financial decision.

Well, debt *is* a big deal. The whole objective of FlexScore is to get people moving in the right direction.

In the case of people with a large amount of debt, there are times when they should consider paying off the debt first before putting anything into the investment world. The high interest rates they are paying for all that debt are greater than the savings interest they would earn through investing. Some financial gurus argue differently. They say you can realize tax breaks and deferrals through the right kinds of savings accounts while simultaneously paying down debt. You can put money into IRAs or 401(k) plans because you defer paying income taxes on money invested in retirement accounts during your income-earning years. Who's correct? It all depends on your individual circumstance.

What is indisputably correct is that having too much debt forces you to make debt payments that rob you of the ability to save money for the future. A feature of FlexScore lets you see how each of these alternatives plays out so you can decide the best way to deal with debt according to your needs. Perhaps you will decide it is best to pay off high interest rate credit cards or loans first and lower-rate cards or loans second. Maybe you will be convinced it is preferable to pay down larger balances first and smaller balances second. FlexScore will show you what gets you the most bang for your buck and in what order so you can keep moving forward financially. We believe the positive momentum you create by making progress you can see is far more important than the specific way you pay down the debt.

"My lifestyle should improve as fast as my wages." People say that to themselves all the time. It's another symptom of financial failure. One would think that the assumption is the more money you make the more, and sooner, you can do the right things financially. But that increase in income won't necessarily solve any problems or bring added happiness. We all like to spend. Corollary assumptions go something like this: I've grown accustomed to my lifestyle; it makes me happy. But now I'm making more money I can go out and do more with an even better lifestyle that will make me even happier.

In fact, there are numerous studies that show an increase of income does not necessarily increase happiness. (See Chapter One, Money Can Make You Happy.) What you should do with that raise or income increase is adopt a save some-spend some mentality. Live on a little more money and save a little more money, but do them together.

You're used to living without that extra money and you admit you're already happy, so saving some of that newfound income shouldn't be a problem. FlexScore helps you understand the value of saving some of that increase in wages or salary because you can go on-line, model your new savings rate and see how much more quickly you will become financially independent.

Volumes have been written about the "The Latte Factor." Various savings masters advocate for it ad nauseam. At its core the Latte Factor is adding up lots of small numbers to equal a large number. It's about how our little habits and indulgences add up to big expenses. Instead of going to Starbucks for that $5 cup of java, put that $5 a day into a savings account. Over your working career, those $5 a day savings will produce a big pot of money. The power of taking so many small numbers and adding them up to benefit you financially is clearly visible by taking a closer look at your monthly debit or credit card statements, specifically all those $3 or $5 items at outfits such as Starbucks. These ingrained habits of seemingly inconsequential amounts we spend and write off as part of life can quickly add up to $100 or more a month. It's not just adding up the small numbers to produce a larger number; it's also how those savings can grow over time based on Einstein's observation about the power of compounding interest.

The principle of the Latte Factor hails from David Bach's recent book, *The Automatic Millionaire: A Powerful One-step Plan to Live and Finish Rich*. He argues that people who don't have money to save or invest waste their money every day on lattes, soda, cigarettes, candy, bottled water and lunches out or buying stuff just to keep up with their peers.

We're sure most of us consider that $5 daily cup of coffee or whatever we're spending money on is worth it at the moment. But now that you know these amounts, invested over 30 years, could turn into a much larger sum, would you trade that minor daily extravagance for what another $150,000 would do in guaranteeing your financial independence during retirement?

"The math behind [commentators such as Bach] is sound, but should you give up your little indulgences?" asks Xin Lu in a 2010 piece published on WiseBread, a blog dedicated to helping people "live large on a small budget." She lays out "reasons why keeping your 'latte factor' will help you save."

First, if you are already putting enough money away into savings then depriving yourself of such "a tiny expense that makes you happy" could become "a negative experience" that will make it "more likely" you will give up on your savings regimen.

Second, saving the few hundred dollars a year represented by giving up on your daily latte "pales in comparison" to much more substantial savings you can realize from such efforts as refinancing your mortgage or all the other measures of reducing your expenses we detailed earlier in this book. "There are many ways you can save without sacrificing anything in your lifestyle, and I think those things should be done before you stop going to Starbucks," Xin Lu points out.

Third, it is a far better idea to use the latte factor to "reward yourself for saving." Spend those small amounts of money on yourself as compensation for hitting your monthly savings goal. Then "you keep your small luxuries as a reminder to save money [and] they will work out to be positive reinforcement."

Saving the small numbers to add up to the large number "is definitely sound," she writes. But the idea that giving up the daily latte will turn you into a millionaire is fundamentally flawed, she concludes, because "those who cut out their morning coffee or newspaper usually do not save that money at all...As long as you are committed to saving consistently, you can build up your nest egg and still keep the small expenditures that enhance your life."

It is up to you to decide. But among the many benefits

FlexScore brings you is the ability to visualize and see the consequences of all of your financial decisions as opposed to just mindlessly spending money.

FlexScore reminds you to pay attention even to the more boring and pedestrian aspects of financial planning such as having the appropriate amount of insurance and estate planning. Just because they're boring doesn't mean they aren't important.

Most people miss the importance of insurance and estate planning until something bad happens and they or their loved ones wish they hadn't. Take estate planning. Many people think it's only for the wealthy. All estate planning comes down to is identifying before you die those things you wish to occur after your death. One of the most vivid examples of the need for estate planning came to us through a company 401(k) plan participant we were advising. He was not in the best of health, was married to his second wife and didn't attempt to conceal his utter hatred for his ex-wife. One day out of the blue we received a phone call from the second wife whom we had never met with the unfortunate news that her husband had passed away. She was anxious to learn how she could get her hands on the money we invested in his retirement plan. Guess who ended up getting the money? Our late client never took the proper steps with his employer to update the beneficiary on his retirement account. All the money went to his very happy ex-wife, much to the chagrin of the second wife.

You get important points from FlexScore for having made adequate arrangements for insurance and estate planning. But if you don't review and, if necessary, update your needs in both of these areas on a frequent enough basis, the points you earn go away. FlexScore forces you to re-examine your life insurance policies and estate planning documents every three to five years to make sure they are accurate and current.

Being too risk-averse in your investments can prevent you from reaching your goals. We learn many important lessons over time from our parents. Financial skills too often aren't among them. Jeff's dad was never educated about investing and therefore didn't believe in it. That is a key reason why Jeff got into this business. How many older clients have we met who only want to put their money into low-yielding CDs? Being afraid to take any risks at all will also ensure financial failure.

Different generations betray different attitudes about the stock market. The generations that survived or grew up during the Great Depression often exhibit a very conservative attitude towards investing money in stocks. The next generation, the Baby Boomers, had a greater willingness to invest in stocks and bonds, and see them as opportunities to grow their fortunes. The generations that followed, including the "Y" and "Z" generations, have not had as much of a positive experience with the stock market; they sometimes use those experiences as an excuse for not saving, much to their own detriment.

Another factor preventing people from investing or causing them to invest in the wrong kinds of stocks are family histories with the markets, good or bad. The relentless noise from the financial media is another factor: You can tune into the financial news and come up with good reasons to invest and good reasons not to invest. This only sows confusion among typical news consumers and leads many of them not to invest at all or to fall victim to reckless investment behaviors.

Being afraid of risk prevents you from making sound financial decisions. Different people have different appetites for taking risk based on their personalities and psychological make-ups; everyone's appetite is legitimate. FlexScore helps you identify your own tolerance for risk and recommends investment portfolios based on that tolerance. FlexScore helps you feel comfortable with what you've done because it is customized to you.

Another serious mistake is ignoring your finances altogether. Too many people believe that if they ignore their finances things will get better or take care of themselves eventually. Nice hope, but not likely. Ignoring reality will only ensure that you fail to reach your financial goals.

How much does the ostrich miss when he buries his head in the sand? Everything. Ignorance is not bliss; it's just ignorance. You can choose not to pay attention, and it is a choice, because the subject is scary or because you think you have to be smarter than you are or be more educated or have more money or because you will have to take the time to pay attention. None of these are good reasons not to pay attention by ignoring your finances.

Spending just a little time learning about something so important as your own money will serve you very well on the long term.

Because FlexScore is so personalized, it focuses you on those things that are most important in your financial life today through the concrete and bite-sized action steps it recommends. In addition, FlexScore's on-line Learning Center will help educate you in plain English about what you need to know to make good decisions. You even earn points on your score by spending time in the Learning Center sections. Numerous studies have demonstrated that financial literacy breeds financial success.

CHAPTER ELEVEN

Success Stories of FlexScore in Action

"Everyone is different. Sometimes it's very exciting and sometimes very scary."

--Emanuel Ax, Polish pianist

Every episode of "Dragnet," the 1950s radio and television crime show staring Jack Webb, began with this disclaimer: "The story you are about to hear is true. Only the names have been changed to protect the innocent."

This final chapter is designed to help readers identify with the success stories of FlexScore by finding themselves in the real life examples we use. These accounts are usually taken from composites of the many clients we have assisted over the years. As the Dragnet reference indicates, we have refrained from using actual client names and have changed some of the facts to protect their privacy. Nevertheless, we have endeavored to include a variety of examples that should fit or be similar to the circumstances of most people who need financial planning advice. Hopefully, you will find people who remind you of yourself in one or more of these examples.

You're going to meet six people in the pages of this section. Their circumstances resemble elements we believe are common to average Americans in the four age categories when it comes to their personal finances.

Among other benefits, FlexScore offers an individualized performance report as to how well you've done with your personal finances. Married people typically combine their finances when it comes to spending and investment choices, and setting common goals and objectives for the future. Having said that, there is no such thing as a joint FlexScore on behalf of a couple. Think of it in the same way that each individual has his or her own FICO© credit score based on the individual's history of credit decisions that rank the person on his or her own scale. When people come together in marriage, one individual can enter information for both spouses, including all the financial details of what they owe and own. But they will each have their own score because there are always differences, even minor, from past histories and even present deficiencies that may differ, such as the amount of life or disability insurance each spouse needs.

We will present you with the stories of individuals comprising various age ranges and financial situations, starting with a young married couple and leaving for last a couple that is now retired. Keep in mind when you examine these examples that score improvement is based on your life situation. Also remember that if you are the principle breadwinner in the family, it will be your obligation to put the most money away for the future and to do more of the paperwork by, say, working with the HR director or financial advisor at your company to commit to a retirement program it offers.

Since FlexScore looks at the household situation rather than the individual family member, many of the questions that are raised will apply to the entire household and not just to the individual using FlexScore in his or her own name.

In this chapter you will meet the following people.

Alan is a 27-year old professional recently married, with no children. He is in office equipment sales, has just started this new career and has been putting money into a 401(k) plan from a past employer for a few years. He is adamant about starting his life on the right financial footing.

Lydia is a 35-year old professional events planner. She's busy with work as well as managing her family, which includes two young children. She's married and is the main breadwinner.

Angelica, at 57, is married with two adult children. She is a tenured professor at the local community college. Angelica and her husband eagerly look forward to retirement and are concerned they may not be as prepared as they hoped they would have been 10 years earlier.

Robert is in his mid-60s, retired and living with his wife. They have three grown children and four grandchildren. The biggest concern of Robert and his wife is running out of money before they run out of life. They also hope to be able to have enough financial horsepower to help their grandchildren pay for college.

In addition, we're going to examine the cases of two men in their mid-40s, **Freddy Frivolous** and **Ricky Responsible**. They look to the outside observer remarkably similar when considering their incomes and lifestyles. But in reality they boast dramatically different financial lives that have earned them their respective handles.

This chapter is organized in the following way: First, we detail each of the six people's financial history, including the goals they have set for themselves. Then we assign them a FlexScore based on the situation we have highlighted. These descriptions will be set out in both text and graphic form.

Second, we will explain how FlexScore sets them on the right path or builds on what they've already achieved, demonstrating how their FlexScore will change after they accomplish their action steps, again in both text and graphic form.

It is important to remember that even if all the action steps these scenarios present are realized, people must be aware that maintaining their financial fitness is much like maintaining their physical fitness. Eating well and exercising regularly are ongoing habits of a lifetime that need to be observed. Similarly, there are numerous small and large action steps that FlexScore will constantly remind you about in order to keep your financial health in good shape and on track.

Meet Alan, a young professional just recently married. His wife moved into the apartment he rents in Atlanta, Georgia. They do not yet have any children but plan on kids after they get used to life as a married couple. She has a full time job as a sales clerk at the corner coffee café, but makes only $10.50 an hour with no benefits. Alan, who sells office equipment, earns $65,000 a year and believes his job provides him with good opportunities for advancement down the road.

Alan and his wife are not financially unlike other young couples as they haven't yet built up a lot of assets. In fact, they already have quite a bit more debt that assets. Alan is paying back a student loan to the tune of $20,000. His credit card debt amounts to $2,000. His wife has credit card debt of $3,000. Their combined checking and savings account balances equal $5,000.

Alan made a good decision when he got his first job at age 20 to begin putting money into a 401(k) plan at work. He has accumulated $10,000 in that account. He was also fortunate that his employer offered to contribute 3 percent of Alan's income each year into the plan; Alan contributes another 5 percent of his income, which has produced the current balance of $10,000.

Alan and his wife share a short-term goal of doing some traveling over the next two years while at the same time increasing what they are saving for potential emergencies. Their mid-term goal within the following two to seven years is buying a home and becoming debt free except for their home mortgage payments, and having children. In the long term, which means more than seven years into the future, Alan and his spouse would like to retire at age 62, with a monthly net income of $7,500. The couple is hoping to benefit from the Social Security system by the time they retire; if it still exists at that time, they will consider it icing on the cake.

Alan harbors a sneaking suspicion they are spending too much each month and should find a way to pay down debt in a more disciplined manner. While coming to this insight, Alan still wants to be able to travel and prepare for babies and a home purchase, but he feels he and his wife have too many competing goals, some of which may conflict with each other. He is looking to figure out what is possible and how they can get started down a new path.

Also on Alan's mind is the fact he has been investing for seven years in his retirement plan and feels his moderately aggressive tolerance for risk differs dramatically from his wife, who has no investment experience and typically makes more conservative financial decisions. "Honey, I'm afraid you're taking too many risks with our money," she has expressed to him. Alan knows that to grow their money he needs to take some risks and as a young couple they have a lot of time on their side.

Like many young people, Alan wants to know precisely where he stands financially, both compared to his peers and in relation to the stated goals and objectives he and his wife have set out. He hopes FlexScore can bring objective clarity to his financial situation so he and his spouse can agree upon the correct path moving forward. He's also hoping FlexScore will provide the "how-to" action steps of what to do and in which order to do it.

Given his current situation, Alan has earned a FlexScore of 245. That may seem low out of a maximum of 1,000 points, but since the score is meant to represent readiness towards true financial independence, given his age and the relatively short period of time he has spent in his career, Alan hasn't had the ability to save more. In fact, Alan is in the middle of the pack among his contemporaries. He has a lot of room for potential growth. With some guidance and discipline, he has the ability to do very well.

Since this young couple feels overwhelmed by all things financial, one of the first steps in helping Alan and his wife is creating the foundation of financial literacy. The FlexScore Learning Center offers hundreds of articles and a series of videos produced exclusively for FlexScore that can help a young couple like Alan and his spouse grasp extremely complex financial concepts, make them easy to understand and relate them to their own situation. Through FlexScore they will acquire a clear understanding of what the action steps are and why they are taking them.

Our years of experience helping people from all income levels and walks of life have taught us that the rich teach their children how to be rich, the poor teach their children how to be poor and the middle class teaches their children how to be middle class. FlexScore seeks to help alter that paradigm by giving the general public a base of knowledge so people can do better financially. We are convinced that financial literacy equals financial freedom.

How many kids do you know who grew up wealthy and who today are on Food Stamps and welfare? There are probably very few, if any. The flip side of that coin is how many poor people who are on Food Stamps, welfare and other public aid are able to break the cycle of poverty and become middle class or even affluent? It does happen, but not often enough.

We recently met and interviewed a young man from a very poor neighborhood in our community who was able to break the cycle of being poor and dependent on government programs. He decided not to follow the path his brother took of entering the gang lifestyle. Instead, he finished high school, attended the local community college and graduated with a degree in finance from the nearby California State University campus. After a week working as an intern at our company, he accepted a full time position with a large manufacturing firm in Southern California, where he is doing very well. This is an example of the exception, but unfortunately it is too often just that: an exception.

The conventional wisdom used to be that upward mobility was much more difficult to achieve in traditional Western European societies than in the United States. People in European countries were destined to fill the jobs or occupations their parents or grandparents worked, if you followed this thinking. Americans liked to boast that in this country you could go beyond what your father or grandfather did.

Recent studies show there is more equality of incomes and more economic mobility in Western Europe than in the U.S. According to a February 2012 article by Timothy Noah, a senior editor at The New Republic magazine and author of the book *The Great Divergence: America's Growing Inequality Crisis and What We Can Do About It*, "it isn't just Western Europe. Countries as varied as Japan, New Zealand, Singapore, and Pakistan all have higher degrees of income mobility than we do. A nation that prides itself on its lack of class rigidity has, in short, become significantly more economically rigid than many other developed countries."

There are plenty of reasons. But part of the problem is the state of financial illiteracy plaguing most Americans. That needs to change.

Boosting financial literacy among Americans is an important step forward. Since all the studies confirm financial literacy translates into financial success, Alan and his wife earn five FlexScore points for viewing the very brief (one to two minute) videos in the FlexScore Learning Center. Material found in the Learning Center will be an ongoing aide to them as they progress through the FlexScore process.

Next, Alan and his wife got together to more clearly define their goals. For example, they want to retire at 62 with no debt, including paying off their home mortgage, and have enough money to supply a $7,500 monthly income. Setting specific financial goals will earn Alan and his spouse valuable FlexScore points. FlexScore showed them that if they increase the amount of debt they pay off each month by $250, they would be done paying off all their debts in less than five years rather than their current path that wouldn't see them eliminating the debt for another 10 years. Not only does the shorter time frame save them interest payments, but it also allows the couple to jumpstart savings for a home purchase.

Based on their goal of receiving $7,500 a month upon retirement, Alan and his wife need to start putting away 19.6 percent of their monthly income into retirement investments. That comes out to $1,330 a month of their current income. They asked that FlexScore not consider Social Security benefits as part of their retirement income stream because they are planning conservatively and are skeptical that Social Security will produce benefits for them when they are ready to stop working.

If Alan and his spouse decide to wait even one more year before putting money away for their future, instead of 19.6 percent, they will need to contribute 21.4 percent of their monthly income, or $1,454 a month instead of $1,330. Imagine how much more they will have to put away if they delay saving for retirement for another five years? The longer you wait to save for retirement the least likely you will be able to retire on your own terms.

By clearly laying out financial options and choices based on what people set as their own goals, FlexScore helps couples avoid one of the most common emotional arguments in their lives, which is over money. FlexScore presents objective background information that both partners must accept because it is founded on the particulars of their own circumstances and stated goals. FlexScore also offers viable and sensible alternatives.

For example, Alan's wife makes $10.50 an hour working 30 hours a week. She may wish to consider two possibilities to provide the household with additional income that will help them achieve their financial goals more quickly: increase her hours to 40 a week or acquire additional skills that will enable her to obtain a higher-paying job. Or she could do both. The magic of FlexScore is that it shows you what you need to do financially in order to meet your goals. How you adjust to meet those goals, such as Alan's wife taking on more hours, is up to the user.

The couple worries that they don't know what it will take for them to reach their other goals. So FlexScore will help them visualize the correct road down which to travel. Other precise action steps they need to take are debt consolidation, which involves combining their multiple credit card balances and student loan debt into one loan boasting a lower interest rate. This will lower their monthly payments so they can free up more money towards paying down their total debt, which will see the couple eliminating it altogether within a shorter period of time.

Another action step is establishing an emergency fund for unplanned costs. At a minimum it should be comprised of three months worth of living expenses in the event of job loss, injury or unanticipated expenses such as major auto or home repairs. Some of our clients have nicknamed this the "Uh-oh" fund.

Obtaining and reviewing their current credit scores is another action step. Their ambition is to buy a home in the near future and they need to make sure their credit report is accurate. If there are any negative issues in the report they can work towards clearing them up and thereby increase their credit score, which will make it easier to qualify for a home loan at a lower interest rate and with more favorable terms.

Every tax time, Alan and his wife are surprised with a bill for about $1,200 due to underpayment of federal taxes, requiring them to fork over money to the IRS. FlexScore tells them to increase their monthly tax withholding on their W-4 forms so they pay enough in taxes throughout the year and avoid a surprise lump sum tax liability in April. It's easier to pay $50 more each paycheck than a big bill of $1,200 once a year. Alternatively, if Alan begins to put more into his company retirement plan, which is already recommended, he'll be able to shelter more current income from taxes since qualified plans like a 401(k) allow for tax deductible contributions.

The following table is a summary of the financial situation for Alan, depicting his before and after financial picture as well as the FlexScore points he is awarded for making progress.

Alan's Household 27 Years Old	Before	After	Points?
Annual Income	$82,000	$88,000	0
Annual Expenses (except for debt payments and savings)	$70,500	$68,000	0
Annual Consumer Debt Payments	$7,500 with an average APR of 13%	$10,000 with an average APR of 6%	25
Annual Savings	$4,000	$10,000	50
Life Insurance	$0 death benefit	$250,000 death benefit	24
Disability Insurance	0	0	0
Investment Risk	9 out of 10	7 out of 10	12
Credit Score Monitoring	No	Yes	7
Estate Planning	No Will	Completed Will	24
Articles and Videos	Financial Literacy = Pre-School	Financial Literacy = Elementary	20
FlexScore™	245	407	+162

Now let us introduce you to Lydia. At 35, she has built up a successful small business as an events planner in a suburb of Seattle, Washington. She divides her time and attention between operating her firm and taking care of her family, including two children, ages seven and four. Her husband is employed full time at a manufacturing facility making $65,000 a year. But she pulls in the majority of the family income, earning $95,000 annually.

Lydia has been able to put away $70,000 in the 401(k) account Lydia created from her business. She has a joint investment brokerage account owned by both her and her husband of $100,000. The husband has $50,000 in his company retirement plan. The couple has $20,000 in their bank savings account and a balance in their joint checking account that dramatically fluctuates depending on the day of the month, but averages $7,000.

They own a home with a $150,000 mortgage. She has an outstanding business loan of $15,000, and they have auto loans adding up to another $15,000. They have no credit card debt, which is a good thing.

Lydia has the mindset of a planner, both professionally and by nature. She is very efficient and wants to use all the pieces of advice and tools available to make their financial lives as easy as possible so she can focus on doing what she enjoys. She is the main financial decision maker in the family and has convinced her husband that they have worked hard long enough so they deserve an upgrade in their standard of living.

She's worked with several financial advisors who frankly concentrated on different aspects of her personal finances, including an insurance agent, a certified public accountant who sells investments and the "investment guy" who handles her business' 401(k) plan. The advice she has received is all well meaning, but she doesn't feel any single part of it is enough to satisfy the worry that her financial situation is still in search of solutions that are comprehensive and holistic.

Her motivation in turning to FlexScore is to fashion an objective plan that helps her three existing financial advisors understand the other aspects of her finances and act accordingly in their individual disciplines based on the priorities she sets through FlexScore.

Finally, she seeks a "sanity check" because although Lydia feels she is doing just fine financially, she doesn't want to behave like a lemming, blindly making financial judgments like many of the people she knows, and perhaps some day finding herself falling off a financial cliff.

Lydia's FlexScore starts out at 475 out of 1,000. To her surprise that is slightly below average compared to her peers. As we'll discover, the reason her score is below average is because Lydia is akin to the person who goes shopping at the grocery store while she's hungry. Her appetite is bigger than her needs; she has oversized her goals. Given her present financial status, Lydia's goals are much more ambitious than her ability to fund them. She's committed to those goals and will have to work a little harder to achieve them or be compelled to redefine what she wishes to accomplish.

The short-term goals Lydia and her husband have set for the next two years are remodeling and upgrading their kitchen with hopes of preparing the house for sale at some point in the next 24 months. Their mid-term goal, between two and seven years from now, is to move to the country on a larger piece of land and to expand her business. Their long-term goal, seven years hence, is to pay for their children's college education and stop working some day, which means they haven't set a specific time or amount of money they need for retirement.

Based on her stated goals and what we know about her financial situation, FlexScore has determined Lydia doesn't have adequate life insurance coverage. She has a policy that would pay $250,000 upon her demise. One action step is purchasing additional life insurance in order to produce added benefits of $525,000, giving her a total death benefit of $775,000.

She is dismayed to learn that one out of three persons will suffer a disability lasting longer than 90 days and that one in 10 will become permanently disabled prior to the age of 65, according to Burton T. Beam Jr.'s textbook, *Group Benefits, Basic Concepts and Alternatives*. Lydia has no disability insurance. FlexScore reveals that without the regular income from her business, household expenses would exceed monthly income by $3,483 a month. One of her action steps is very simple: Acquire sufficient disability insurance.

One of Lydia's identified goals is putting her kids through college. With college costs increasing at twice the rate of inflation, it's important to start saving early, while her children are still young. It's better to have interest in a regular savings program working for her than having interest work against her down the road in the form of having to pay off student loans. The amount needed for Lydia to meet her goal of paying the college costs of her offspring is $363,898. She would need to save $935 a month and increase her rate of savings by 3 percent a year to accumulate that much money by the time her kids are ready for college. Or she could invest a lump sum of $160,000, which she doesn't currently have.

Although funding college is a noble goal, fulfilling it in practice may seriously impede Lydia's capacity to achieve her longer-term goal of personal retirement. She may want to reconsider covering the entire costs of college education and instead subsidize part of it, leaving the children to consider working during their college years or applying for student loans and scholarships.

Lydia's total business and auto debt equals $30,000. At an average annual interest rate of 10 percent and monthly payments of $500, that debt will be paid off in seven years. FlexScore says she should consider debt consolidation that could result in a new single loan with a lower interest rate and quicker payoff.

Her final action step is the big one: How much money does she need to save each month to accomplish her goal of some day retiring? Part of her goal setting has to embrace bringing more clarity and detail to the decision making, which includes an actual amount on which she and her husband can comfortably live in retirement when it comes at the right time.

Based on current income for Lydia and her husband, and assuming they will need to live on 70 percent of that income during retirement, that they will ideally earn an 8 percent return on their investments and that both spouses will benefit from Social Security, Lydia and her husband need to save 18 percent of their yearly income, or $2,500 a month, in order to retire at age 65. They are also counting on her husband's employer to continue to make generous contributions to his company retirement plan account by way of contribution matching and profit sharing.

The following table is a summary of the financial picture for Lydia, depicting her before and after financial situation as well as the FlexScore points she is awarded for making progress.

Lydia's Household 35 Years Old	Before	After	Points?
Annual Income	$160,000	$160,000	0
Annual Expenses (except for debt payments and savings)	$135,000	$120,000	0
Annual Consumer Debt Payments	$6,000 with an average APR of 10%	$10,000 with an average APR of 7%	25
Annual Savings	$19,000	$30,000	40
Life Insurance	$250,000 death benefit	$775,000 death benefit	15
Disability Insurance	0	Policy for 70% Income Replacement	36
Investment Risk	5 out of 10	7 out of 10	12
Annual College Savings	0	$5,000	10
Estate Planning	Has Will	Reviewed / Updated Will	16
Articles and Videos	Financial Literacy = Elementary	Financial Literacy = Jr. High	15
FlexScore™	475	644	+169

Now make the acquaintance of Angelica, 57, married with two adult offspring. She has earned tenure as a professor of English at a community college in Boston, Massachusetts. Her husband, who is 60, teaches high school physical education. They are homeowners. Neither of them have 401(k) plans that are more common in the corporate world. However, they both have 403(b) plans, similar to 401(k) accounts. In addition, they are both fortunate to have defined benefit pension plans through the public institutions that employ them, which means they'll have a guaranteed retirement income stream other than Social Security. Because they've never worked outside of public education, neither one of them has paid into Social Security so they won't realize any of its benefits.

The husband has $125,000 in his 403(b) plan; Angelica has $175,000 in her account. They have a joint investment brokerage account worth about $200,000. Their home mortgage is $350,000. Combined car loans amount to $25,000. There is $15,000 in credit card debt divided among the three cards they hold between them. They have very little in a bank savings account and carry an average joint checking account balance of about $8,000. They own a nice sailboat that is kept at a local marina and regularly enjoy taking it out.

Their short-term goals are to retire within two years and to move closer to their grandchildren in Texas. The mid-term goal is to travel after retirement and pursue their hobbies, which include boating and shopping for and collecting antiques in addition to performing volunteer work in the community. Long term they want to leave an inheritance of at least $250,000 to each of their two adult children.

What is Angelica's motivation for using FlexScore? She and her husband know these are their goals. They're not sure if they are reasonable goals. Will they have enough money to achieve their dreams? Do they have more dreams than money to pay for them? They seek to validate the advice they've received in the past as to how their money is currently invested and be reassured they will soon be able to retire.

Their FlexScore is 825, which is good. It appears they are on track to being financially independent. They can get as close as possible with a few tweaks.

Since Angelica wants to retire in two years, FlexScore examined her retirement resources. Because both she and her husband are educators with publicly financed pensions they probably have enough income to see them through. But her long-term goal is to leave at least $250,000 in liquid assets to each of their two children. The dilemma is this: If they want to move to Texas in the near term, they are slightly upside down on their home; it is worth somewhat less than the balance on the mortgage. This means they need to pay down the mortgage, which would leave them with less financial wiggle room for the present. Maintaining a high credit score is important to the couple and they feel an obligation to repay the debt they borrowed. So a "short sale" of the home, where a homeowner is allowed by the mortgage lender to sell the home for less than what is owed, is not an option in their minds.

Because of their age, one of the first recommendations suggested by FlexScore is acquiring long-term care insurance so they can fulfill the long-term goal of leaving assets to their children. This insurance covers medical and convalescent care for people who can no longer perform the basic personal activities of daily life such as bathing, dressing and feeding themselves. It provides both in-home and in-facility care; more limited policies cover only in-facility care. Because of Angelica's goal of bequeathing money to her children upon her death, she sees long term care insurance as protecting their inheritance.

The risk tolerance Angelica inputted into FlexScore is four on a 10-point scale with 10 being more aggressive. They haven't paid much attention to their investment portfolios because they are relying on their public pensions. They always considered the portfolios as extra money. Angelica chose four out of 10 because it's always bothered her that her money swings so dramatically up and down with the markets; she's never been emotionally comfortable with the fluctuations.

Her investment advisor has just told her to stay the course and everything will be okay. The risk position of her actual portfolio is eight out of 10 on the scale. So FlexScore recommends a more suitable mix of investments that would take no more risk than Angelica feels comfortable assuming.

Angelica did not explicitly create a goal of becoming debt free via FlexScore, even as she desires to do so. Since her goal is to retire within a few years, the more conservative route of becoming debt free in retirement is highly desirable, except for the home mortgage that many people take into retirement. FlexScore's recommendation is to allocate an extra $500 a month to pay off the existing $25,000 in car loans and the $15,000 in credit card debt in less than three years instead of five years. That is the route they are on now. In addition, FlexScore suggests options to consolidate the debt into one loan with a lower interest rate, which will aid paying it off sooner.

Finally, Angelica needs to also update her will. She has listed a specific desire to bequeath assets to her children. FlexScore recommends the will update as part of her intake profile since it has been more than 10 years since she last examined it. Circumstances and resources change; wills need to be reviewed and updated to reflect changing desires and realities.

The following table is a summary of the financial situation for Angelica, depicting her before and after financial picture as well as the FlexScore points she is awarded for making progress.

Angelica's Household 57 Years Old	Before	After	Points?
Annual Income	$160,000	$160,000	0
Annual Expenses (except for debt payments and savings)	$145,000	$139,000	0
Annual Consumer Debt Payments	$9,000 with an average APR of 11%	$15,000 with an average APR of of 8%	25
Annual Savings	$6,000	$6,000	0
Life Insurance	$300,000	$300,000	0
Long Term Care Insurance	$0 Daily Benefit	$200 Daily Benefit	32
Investment Risk	8 out of 10	4 out of 10	12
Credit Score Monitoring	No	Yes	7
Estate Planning	No Will	Reviewed / Updated Will	20
Articles and Videos	Financial Literacy = High School	Financial Literacy = High School	0
FlexScore™	825	921	+96

Now meet Robert, who is retired and living in the San Francisco Bay Area. He is 67. His wife is 63. They have three grown children and four grandchildren, ages two, five, seven and 11. In order to fund the lifestyle to which they have become accustomed, Robert and his wife regularly take withdrawals out of their retirement investments: $17,000 a month gross, $12,500 net after taxes. He receives Social Security income of $1,800 a month. At 63, Robert's wife is trying to decide whether to take her Social Security now or wait until later when she would receive a larger benefit.

Their monthly consumer debt is zero. They are not currently saving any money each month because they are now retired and in a "spend down" and not an "accumulation" mode. Their IRA accounts total $1.75 million. They also have an after-tax joint investment brokerage account (money they saved outside of their retirement plans) of $160,000. Their home is worth $1.2 million and they have a $400,000 mortgage that was recently refinanced at a 15-year fixed rate; their new payment is $3,000 a month for shelter. (This may seem like a lot of money for housing to most Americans, but it is median-sized in the notoriously expensive Bay Area.) They have no life insurance and no long-term care insurance.

The goal of Robert and his wife is to live comfortably for the rest of their lives without worrying about running out of money before they run out of life. They also want to help cover the costs of college education for their young grandchildren, as they did for their own children. In addition, they want to continue enjoying their hobbies that include season tickets to the theater, the San Francisco Giants major league baseball team, their annual luxurious cruise vacation that includes the entire family and regular visits to the nearby California Wine Country.

Robert is looking to FlexScore to confirm that he and his spouse are going to be all right financially, which is what they have always believed. Before FlexScore, Robert was convinced he was set in his life, that he had way more money than he needed.

However, upon completing the FlexScore process, Robert is

Jason Gordo & Jeff Burrow

blown away to discover that his score is only 785, well below the average for his peers. The primary reason is that the amount of cash he and his wife are spending each month will cause them to run out of money in less than 10 years, given what they are realizing on their investments. Since they are both relatively healthy, their current rate of spending will likely leave them with no financial resources and plenty of life left to live. If this couple does nothing and keeps on its present spending course there are serious troubles ahead.

FlexScore says the critical action step is for Robert to immediately reduce his annual spending which is drawing down his nest egg. Robert and his spouse have lived a life of affluence for a long time. In order to be able to continue spending what they're currently withdrawing ($17,000 a month), prior to retirement they should have accumulated another $650,000. They really retired too early. Now they either need to downsize their lifestyle or go back to work, which is probably not an option.

Coming up with more money is too big a hurdle for most people in Robert's situation. If he had been aware of this reality earlier he could have worked a little longer to build up more of a nest egg. Then he and his wife would have been living off of their earnings from his occupation rather than taking principal out of their investments. Also remember, you never know in any given year whether your portfolio will suffer a market loss, albeit a temporary one.

That means if you retire too soon, you could be faced with having to survive too many years on your nest egg without any other source of income. You can plan early on to reduce that risk by deciding to save a little extra each month so you can retire earlier and with a larger nest egg. If you are nearing retirement and realize you don't have enough invested, one strategy is to work a little longer. That lets your nest egg earn more interest. It gives you additional time to contribute savings towards it. And more than likely it reduces the number of years you'll need to draw upon your savings.

FlexScore provides the tools to determine what's the best course. It could have saved Robert no small amount of worry once he appreciated the reality he was facing.

To rectify his dilemma, Robert needs to reduce his monthly income withdrawal from $17,000 to $13,750, or by $3,250 a month. This is where the rubber meets the road. Numbers don't lie. Despite the fact Robert has accumulated quite a bit of money, he has been super-sizing his lifestyle. It's a problem people with much more modest means also face.

Robert has some options. Instead of season tickets to the Giants, he can purchase tickets to particular games he wants to see. Instead of that luxurious annual ocean cruise he pays for the entire family to take, including children, their spouses and grandchildren, Robert and his wife can decide to still have fun together but for a lot less money. If he wants to spoil his children and grandchildren, he can do it in ways that are much less expensive.

As we've stated before the beauty of FlexScore is not that it makes choices for you. It does clearly show you what needs to be done to accomplish your goals. It allows you to have informed conversations with your loved ones on how you can reduce spending and still meet your needs. For someone at Robert's point in life this is one of the biggest challenges: He is no longer trying to save or accumulate assets; he's simply trying to spend enough to have a life worth living but not in a manner that will cause him to deplete his nest egg before his life ends.

Robert's situation is the equivalent of going down the buffet line. The eater's eyes are much bigger than his stomach. Robert believed he was a multi-millionaire and wanted to lead the life and lifestyle he thought a multi-millionaire should lead. Hopefully, after receiving his FlexScore number and taking his action steps, Robert will wake up and figure out he can't continue being the big spender he had become. He happens to have a lot of money and some issues that need resolving. This phenomenon can plague people at any financial level.

People come to believe the amount of money they have earned is a lot when it isn't nearly enough to carry them comfortably through the rest of their lives. Someone looks at a nest egg of $650,000; that seems like a good pot of money. But as we've repeatedly demonstrated in this book, it's not if you're relying on it to fund the rest of your days given how modern medical science has greatly increased life spans. In 1930, when life expectancy was 68 years of age and the Social Security actuaries who created the system planned on people living an average of six years after retirement, it wasn't a big risk to set eligibility for starting to receive benefits at age 62. Things have dramatically changed since then. What also needs to change is your ability to prepare yourself for an independent financial future.

The following table is a summary of the financial picture for Robert, depicting his before and after financial situation as well as the FlexScore points he is awarded for making progress.

Robert's Household 67 Years Old	Before	After	Points?
Annual Income	$150,000	$165,000	0
Annual Expenses (except for debt payments and savings)	$204,000	$165,000	60
Annual Consumer Debt Payments	$0	$0	0
Annual Savings	$0	$0	0
Life Insurance	0	0	0
Long Term Care Insurance	0	0	0
Investment Risk	5 out of 10	6 out of 10	8
Annual College Savings	0	0	0
Estate Planning	Living Trust	Reviewed and Updated Living Trust	20
Articles and Videos	Financial Literacy = High School	Financial Literacy = University	20
FlexScore™	785	893	+108

The next two people we examine, Freddy and Ricky,

look much the same from the outset. They're the same age, in their mid-40s. They live next door to each other in the same neighborhood in Miami, Florida. They both make $180,000 a year, a very good income. They both have two children and a desire to fund their kids' college educations. They both seek to retire in 15 years at age 60.

But they couldn't be more different.

Freddy Frivolous is an intellectual property attorney, divorced and with two kids, 14 and 17. With his $180,000 income, he earns $15,000 a month gross and brings home $10,500 a month. His 401(k) plan has $125,000 in it. His Roth IRA has another $2,000. His after-tax investment brokerage account holds $5,000.

The mortgage balance on Freddy's "underwater" home is $550,000; it is valued at only $400,000. His monthly mortgage payment is $2,850. His monthly payments on $50,000 of credit card debt amount to $1,000. He also makes monthly payments of $450 toward his $35,000 car loan. His child support payment is $2,228 per month plus $500 a month for health and dental coverage, although this duty will end when his children turn 18. He has neither life nor disability insurance protection.

Freddy's short-term goal is to become debt free except for his home mortgage within the next two years. His mid-term goal is to help his children pay for half of their college expenses within the next two to four years. The long-term goal is to retire with a net income of $10,000 a month at age 60. He wants to leave at least $500,000 to each of his two children.

Even Freddy realizes his life is a financial mess. He wants FlexScore to help tell him all the things he needs to do, what steps he should take first and give him an idea of whether he can even attain his goals within the time frames he has set.

Freddy's FlexScore is 369, which is extremely low for someone of his age and income.

Although he knows he has not exactly done what he should have accomplished financially so far in his life, Freddy believes he can still pull it all together and retire at age 60 because of his high income. FlexScore quickly disabuses him of that notion. It lets him know he actually will not be retiring at any age without adopting some drastic changes. In fact, the answer to the question of how much longer it will take Freddy to prepare to retire, given his monthly income goal at retirement and the current trajectory of his finances, is in 64 more years, when he will be 109 years of age.

Needless to say, Freddy's current plan, which is really no plan at all, is useless. To retire in 15 years, as he desires, FlexScore says the actual amount of money Freddy would need to save is $83,000 this year. It goes up with the rising rate of inflation by 3.5 percent each year. With his current lifestyle costs and obligations, he has zero chance of success.

Freddy's best bet is committing himself to working to a later age. Freddy decides he is willing to work an additional 10 years, until age 70, which gives him 25 more years of work instead of 15. That would make a big difference. He also needs to be able to live on less money today and plan on receiving less in retirement.

The good news is all is not lost. Freddy is still a young man. He does bring home a high income. He has the potential resources to still make things work out, with some big changes.

Given the lump sum amount he's saved to date, which is $132,000, Freddy's moderately aggressive risk tolerance (he's a seven on a scale of 10) and frankly his respectable income, FlexScore says he needs to save $2,100 a month to reach his revised goal of retirement at age 70. That would ideally replace 75 percent of his current income for the rest of his life after quitting work.

There is some other good news and some bad news for Freddy. The good news is in five years, when he's done paying off his debt, he'll free up more than $1,450 a month in cash flow that can switch from debt payments to retirement savings. This will increase the odds of his retirement at age 70.

The bad news is he has five years until he has some wiggle room in his monthly budget in order to make the required monthly retirement contributions. If he doesn't' put away the $2,100 a month and waits five years before contributing, here's what will happen: Five years from now, instead of contributing $2,100 a month, Freddy will need to commit $3,300 a month to make his goal. Will he be able to do that? Possibly. It'll be up to him. That's the power of FlexScore: It doesn't tell you what you have to do; it tells you what you need to do to accomplish your goals as you've defined them.

Freddy's first big challenge is getting a grasp around what his current lifestyle needs should cost him. We deliberately use the word needs, not wants.

The second step is spending only the money he is making from earnings. This means stop spending money on credit. He needs to stop the bleeding.

The third step is committing to and executing paying down his current debt, which amounts to $85,000. To do that Freddy needs to make monthly payments of $1,850. That may sound like a lot of money, but he's now forking over $1,450 a month on debt payments ($1,000 on credit cards and $450 for his auto loan). He only needs to raise it by $400 a month, which is not at all unreasonable considering his income.

Adhering to this regimen would leave him debt free, except for his house, in less than five years, an achievable goal. Like any person with multiple debt accounts, including credit cards, auto and personal loans, there is often an opportunity to consolidate those debts onto a lower interest rate loan. By doing so, you can get committed to a payoff plan that gets you to zero more quickly and with lower interest payments.

One of Freddy's goals is paying for half of his kids' college expenses. He needs to make a decision on whether to further delay or limit his contributions to retirement since having to pay part of the college costs will lessen the amount of money he will have to put towards retiring. An alternative is making the tough decision to accept the hard fact that because Freddy was frivolous during his younger years he will not have the ability to pay much at all of his children's higher education expenses. They will have to rely on other means such as loans, grants and scholarships. Or they can adopt the good old-fashioned approach of working their way through college.

FlexScore will recommend Freddy consider adequate life and disability insurance, but at this point in his life he doesn't have the financial wherewithal to purchase it.

The following table is a summary of the financial situation for Freddy, depicting his before and after financial picture as well as the FlexScore points he is awarded for making progress.

Freddy's Household 45 Years Old	Before	After	Points?
Annual Income	$180,000	$180,000	0
Annual Expenses (except for debt payments and savings)	$155,400	$141,600	0
Annual Consumer Debt Payments	$17,400 with an average APR of 14%	$22,200 with an average APR of 9%	25
Annual Savings	$7,200	$16,200	54
Life Insurance	0	0	0
Disability Insurance	0	0	0
Investment Risk	9 out of 10	7 out of 10	15
Annual College Savings	0	0	0
Estate Planning	Will	Reviewed / Updated Will	24
Articles and Videos	Financial Literacy = Elementary	Financial Literacy = Jr. High	20
FlexScore™	369	507	+138

Freddy's peer and next-door neighbor is, by contrast, Ricky Responsible. In software sales, Ricky is married with two children, ages 12 and 15. He also earns $180,000 a year or $15,000 a month, and takes home $10,500 after taxes. His wife is a homemaker. Ricky has $235,000 in a 401(k) plan, a Roth IRA account worth $72,000, and a joint investment brokerage account amounting to

$80,000.

As Freddy Frivolous' next-door neighbor, Ricky's home is similarly valued at $400,000, but his mortgage is $325,000. Ricky's consumer debt costs total $625 a month. He has no car loan debt. He does have a $1.5 million life insurance policy, but no disability coverage.

Ricky's short-term goal is establishing college savings accounts for his two children and reassuring his wife that he has appropriate insurance protections for his dependents. His 401(k) account has measurably grown, but he knows he has up until now assumed a great deal of risk with his investments and would like to dial them back a little bit. His mid-term goal is to pay for 100 percent of his kids' college costs. The long-term goal is to retire at age 60 with a net monthly after-tax income of $9,000. Like Freddy, he also wants to leave $500,000 to each of his children.

With his disciplined habits and lifestyle, Ricky is looking to FlexScore for confirmation that his financial decisions and current status have placed him in a position to achieve all of his goals. Like many people approaching mid-life, Ricky also harbors a deep curiosity to know how much better he is doing than his peers, especially his neighbor, Freddy Frivolous.

Ricky's FlexScore is 643. In relation to Freddy, he's doing remarkably better given their equality of financial horsepower. Ricky has confirmed he is above average at this time in his life compared with his peers. But he's very disappointed that he's not higher up the chart and that he's only marginally better than those with whom he compares himself (other than Freddy). To Ricky's surprise, he actually hasn't done a good enough job accumulating adequate money to reach his long-term goals.

To receive $9,000 in after-tax monthly income and leave $500,000 to each of his two offspring, he would need a nest egg of $2.9 million upon retirement at age 60. At the moment, Ricky is on track to accumulate about $1.6 million.

That may sound like a lot of money, but it's not enough to

sustain Ricky in the style to which he and his wife have become accustomed or to leave the inheritance for his children. So Ricky needs to put away a total of $2,000 a month to meet his twin goals of retirement and bequests to his kids. That is only $500 more than his current monthly contribution.

Ricky compared himself to his hapless neighbor for so long that he grew complacent and satisfied with his own record of financial success. By doing so he lost sight of what it took to realize his and his wife's personal financial goals. FlexScore allows Ricky to get back on track and to forget about comparing himself to Freddy or anyone else. FlexScore helps Ricky become laser-focused on achieving his own financial ambitions.

When it comes to his investments, FlexScore scans through all of Ricky's holdings and determines the amount of risk he is taking is very high and not close to matching his true risk tolerance. With some adjustments, he will be able to fully align his portfolio with his tolerance for risk, thus earning FlexScore points.

Then there is the goal of assuring his wife that his insurance is adequate. Ricky has appropriate life insurance, but FlexScore recommends he also acquire an adequate disability insurance policy to protect his dependents, which he can afford.

The wife is sleeping better knowing she and their children are fully protected as Ricky is the sole breadwinner in the family.

Finally, since Ricky's children are approaching college age, at 12 and 15, FlexScore indicates that to establish a college fund for each child and contribute enough money to have 100 percent of future college expenses covered would probably take too much away from his contributions toward retirement; Ricky settles for wanting to pay for at least half of their college expenses and will help out as much as he can through monthly cash flow now and in the future.

The following table is a summary of the financial picture for Ricky, depicting his before and after financial situation as well as the FlexScore points he is awarded for making progress.

Ricky's Household 45 Years Old	Before	After	Points?
Annual Income	$180,000	$180,000	0
Annual Expenses (except for debt payments and savings)	$154,500	$148,500	0
Annual Consumer Debt Payments	$7,500 with an average APR of 8%	$7,500 with an average APR of 5%	12
Annual Savings	$18,000	$24,000	37
Life Insurance	$1,500,000 Million Death Benefit	$1,500,000 Million Death Benefit	0
Disability Insurance	0	Policy for 70% Income Replacement	36
Investment Risk	10 out of 10	7 out of 10	20
Annual College Savings	0	$6,000	10
Estate Planning	No Will	Reviewed / Updated Will	24
Articles and Videos	Financial Literacy = High School	Financial Literacy = University	20
FlexScore™	**643**	**802**	**+159**

In these examples, we've seen how a variety of ordinary people of different ages, professions, and income levels all used FlexScore to their advantage. Not everyone can be Ricky Responsible. On the road to financial freedom, we strive to help you from becoming Freddy Frivolous, who jeopardized his retirement goals by spending recklessly and failing to plan for the future. Between these polar opposites reside a range of more typical people such as Alan, Lydia, Angelica and Robert—people with different financial strengths and weaknesses. It's likely that you, too, fall somewhere in this middle ground.

But how do your finances compare? When it comes to managing money, are you closer to a Freddy Frivolous or a Ricky Responsible? The sooner you find out, the sooner you will rectify your plan to guarantee your future and attain the financial independence you desire. FlexScore will show you how. Comprehensive. Personalized. Simple. Understandable. Accessible. Fun.

What's your FlexScore? Find out at www.FlexScore.com.

ABOUT THE AUTHORS

Jeff Burrow, CFP® and Jason Gordo, AIF® began their careers at two different major Wall Street brokerage firms, but over time became disenchanted with the culture of the companies where they worked.

Since the large brokerage houses were created around the paradigm of salesmanship and not stewardship, Jeff and Jason were not able to fully implement their vision of growing and protecting their clients' wealth using the highest levels of ideas and practices they could muster. That is why they co-founded their own California asset management company, Valley Wealth Inc., and later also co-founded FlexScore, based in San Francisco.

In addition, Jason Gordo is a Chartered Retirement Plans Specialist℠ and Accredited Investment Fiduciary®. His responsibilities consist of providing professional money management consulting solutions to retirement plans, institutions and foundations. Jason's clientele are small to mid-size businesses, charitable foundations, wealthy families and professionals.

Jason holds a Bachelor's Degree in Business Management from the University of Phoenix and continued his education by earning credentials from the College for Financial Planning and the Center for Fiduciary Studies. He is proud to be very active in his community. Currently, he is a member of the Modesto Rotary Club, a board member of the Education Foundation of Stanislaus County and on the Board of Trustees for the Gallo Center for the Arts Foundation. Jason is also the current or past community coordinator for The Valley Apprentice and Community Brunch Serving YOUth. Additionally, he is frequently asked to be master of ceremony for numerous community and non-profit group events. He was born and raised in Modesto, California and makes his home with his wife, Tracy, and their three young daughters, Emily, Lily, and Grace.

Jeff Burrow is a CERTIFIED FINANCIAL PLANNER™ practitioner, a Chartered Retirement Plans Specialist℠ and an Accredited Investment Fiduciary.® Jeff focuses on wealth planning and asset management. His clientele consists of company retirement plans, business owners, affluent baby boomers and non-profit organizations.

After graduating with honors from the University of California, Santa Barbara, Jeff also continued his education by earning credentials from the American College, the College for Financial Planning and the Center for Fiduciary Studies. A very active member of his community, Jeff is a past member of the board of directors for the Stanislaus County Estate Planning Council and the Planned Giving Committee of Emanuel Medical Center.

Jeff participated as a Junior Achievement Business Volunteer at middle and high schools, and has been a member of Rotary International's Group Study Exchange to New Zealand for District 5220. Also born and raised in the Central Valley of California, Jeff is happy to live in the same community where he grew up. He and his wife, Nicole, keep busy raising their three children, Bronson, Makayla, and Kendall.